TAKEN SOMEHOW
BY SURPRISE

FOUR LAKES POETRY SERIES

Ronald Wallace, General Editor

TAKEN SOMEHOW
BY SURPRISE

DAVID CLEWELL

THE UNIVERSITY OF WISCONSIN PRESS

The University of Wisconsin Press
1930 Monroe Street, 3rd Floor
Madison, Wisconsin 53711-2059
uwpress.wisc.edu

3 Henrietta Street
London WC2E 8LU, England
eurospanbookstore.com

5   4   3   2   1

Printed in the United States of America

Library of Congress Cataloging-in-Publication Data
Clewell, David, 1955–
   Taken somehow by surprise / David Clewell.
      p. cm. — (Four Lakes poetry series)
Poems.
ISBN 978-0-299-25114-7 (pbk. : alk. paper) — ISBN 978-0-299-25113-0 (e-book)
I. Title. II. Series: Four Lakes poetry series.
PS3553.L42T34 2011
811'.54—dc22
                              2010046334

Book design: Alcorn Publication Design

for Patricia and Ben,
with whom I'm so unsurprisingly taken every day . . .

and in memory of my brother-in-offbeat-arms, Connor Shaw, jazz drummer and
reader extraordinaire:
"Yeah, you're right, Cool—it's an amazing world again."

❖ CONTENTS ❖

❧ ACKNOWLEDGMENTS ❧

Grateful acknowledgment is made to the editors of the following publications where many of
these poems first appeared:

Boulevard: "The Accomplice"

The Georgia Review: "Albert Einstein Held Me in His Arms"; "This Poem Had Better
Be about the World We Actually Live In"; "Uncle Bud, Unshaken in the Wake of
Sputnik: October 1957"

MARGIE/American Journal of Poetry: "The Flamingos Have Left the Building"; "Home
Movies of the Space Race"; "No More Mail from Baltimore"; "Not Exactly Rocket
Science"

Natural Bridge: "The Only Time There Is"

New Letters: "The All-Dressed-Up-and-Going-Nowhere Ghosts"; "A Brief History of the
Moon in Twentieth-Century Song, and Then Some"; "Goodbye to the Blockhead";
"How the Visiting Poet Ended Up in the Abandoned Nike Missile Silo in Pacific,
Missouri, after Surviving a Morning of Grade-School Classroom Appearances on
Behalf of One of the Better Impulses in the History of Human Behavior"

New Ohio Review: "In My Dream, Coleman Hawkins"

River Styx: "A Pocket Guide to Trouble"

Third Coast: "All Night and Always"; "So Much Gone and Going"

TriQuarterly: "The Perfect Stranger"

WordVirtual.com: "The Chicago Cowboy" (excerpts); "The Difference a Day Makes"
(excerpts)

"The Accomplice" was published in *The Conspiracy Quartet* (Garlic Press).

"Albert Einstein Held Me in His Arms" was reprinted on the *Poetry Daily* website
(www.poems.com), in the online version of *Discover* (www.discovermagazine.com),

and in *The Ultimate Quotable Einstein*, edited by Alice Calaprice (Princeton
University Press).

"How the Visiting Poet Ended Up . . ." was reprinted on the *Poetry Daily* website.

"Jack Ruby's America" was published in a limited edition by Garlic Press.

"Jack Ruby Talks Business with the New Girl" was published in *The Low End of Higher
Things* (University of Wisconsin Press).

"Maybe Just One Poem in This Fecund Spring . . ." was included in *Observable Readings:
2006–2007* (Observable Books).

"A Pocket Guide to Trouble" was reprinted in *Seriously Funny: Poems about Love, Death,
Religion, Art, Politics, Sex, and Everything Else*, edited by Barbara Hamby and David
Kirby (University of Georgia Press).

"This Poem Had Better Be about the World We Actually Live In" was reprinted in *The
Best American Poetry 2010*, edited by David Lehman and Amy Gerstler (Scribner).

In addition to the aforementioned editors, a small handful of assiduous civilian-readers egged
me on: Murray Farish, Pete Genovese, the late Dave Hilton, Ron Koertge, David Lee, Dale
Woolery . . . and especially Patricia—she of the unerring eye and ear—who never fails to help
me measure up, word by precarious word. In all but a single instance, I took her word for a
better one; probably I should have turned "angora" into "cashmere," too. Readers should feel
free to nod and make that substitution when they get there.

Special thanks to the dean of Webster University's College of Arts & Sciences, David Wilson,
for his generous support of the eccentric research that underpins several of these poems.

My gratitude also to the folks at the University of Wisconsin Press, especially Katie Malchow
in acquisitions, who expertly shepherded the manuscript early on, and editor Adam Mehring,
whose careful attention and spirited commentary provided me with a copyedited manuscript
that was a real pleasure to respond to. With genuine grace and good humor, these two put up
with one compulsive writer—and lived to tell about it, no doubt . . .

And here, now textured like a blotter, like the going years
And difficult to see, is where you are, and where I am,
And where the oceans cover us.
    —Weldon Kees, "Travels in North America"

Taken Somehow by Surprise

The Accomplice

This poem isn't an intricate theory years in the making.
This poem can speak only for this poem.
This poem will tell you it's not what you think.
This poem is nothing more than a series of coincidences.
This poem can't help but attract the occasional crackpot.
This poem is offered in full compliance with the Freedom of Information Act.
This poem is not anything like the Official Version.
This poem is holding something back.
This poem is covering up.
This poem may be afraid of worldwide panic.
This poem is no secret prototype the government is testing.

This poem has a lot of powerful friends behind it.
This poem is something you'd be happier not knowing.
This poem is murder on reliable eyewitnesses.
This poem is counting on your complete cooperation.
This poem can put you at the scene of untold crimes, or
this poem is your iron-clad alibi, depending.
This poem doesn't want anything to happen to you.
This poem hopes you get the message, although
this poem has no explicit message of its own.
This poem can't promise it will bail you out.
This poem won't even remember you.
This poem is well aware of the statute of limitations.

This poem means what it says.

This poem means anything you need it to.

This poem has seen things hard to believe.

This poem is all you have to believe.

This poem has implications.

This poem couldn't possibly be.

This poem is so good it ought to be illegal.

This poem is the only hard evidence recovered.

This poem has your prints all over it.

This poem has recently been discharged.

This poem is not a disgruntled loner acting spontaneously.

This poem has been seen consorting with other known poems.

This poem has confederates in top-floor windows all over the city.

This poem never goes by the same name twice.

This poem has no highly trained Russian look-alike.

This poem never received specific instructions.

This poem has nothing better to do.

This poem can hit you where you live.

This poem seldom misses at this distance.

This poem has its story down cold.

This poem doesn't want to have to say it more than once.

This poem has never seen its share of the money.

This poem is just the patsy.

This poem laughs at the Witness Protection Program.

This poem wants immunity before it starts naming names.

This poem isn't taking the fall for anyone.

This poem has you exactly where it wants you.

This poem you think you're getting to the bottom of right now,
this poem that's taken you into its confidence,
this poem that's made you an accomplice-after-whatever-the-fact,
this poem suggesting in so many words that it's always been on your side:

this poem doesn't make those kinds of mistakes.
This poem will give you up every time.

Somewhere Else We Have to Be

*Just tell your hoodlum friend outside
you ain't got time to take a ride.*
—The Coasters, *Yakety-Yak*

This Poem Had Better Be about the World We Actually Live In

i. There's No Chance of a Proper Introduction to the World—

not given how we usually enter into it headfirst, crying
and pissing and, if not exactly stunned, then wide-eyed in the sudden light
and hungry most of all. Even before we know who we are, we call the world
by its first name, which not so surprisingly turns out to be
whatever we think we have coming. And doesn't that seem a little
unreasonably familiar, considering the formal, ages-old arrangement:
we take our small place here, already squirming; we have to vacate the premises
whenever the lease is up. We're signing on before we can manage even
two real words in a row, but hey—we know the world when we see it.
And when we say its name, we're so alive it hurts, already
wishing it could stay said that inchoate way forever.

ii. A Study Guide in Middle Age

There's no more relying on the first name of the world.
Now it goes by pseudonyms, aliases, guises and disguises, AKAs
for all occasions, schoolyard nicknames, epithets, and honorary titles.
And because there's no way you can hope to be encyclopedic,
here are just a few of those it wouldn't hurt to learn, remarkably
suitable in a variety of situations:

Fred. Kilroy. Ichabod. Cinquain-crazy Adelaide Crapsey.
Larson E. Whipsnade. The Little Tramp. Dewey, Cheatham, & Howe.

He who laughs last is slow to catch on. There will be a test on this.

Too Much With Us, Late and Soon. Late to Supper. Walk-ins Welcome.
God's Whoopee Cushion. The Runaway Train. All Hat and No Cattle.

You can know by heart more names for the world than anyone alive,
but you still can't take it with you.

Rough and Tumble. Wash & Wear. No Shoes, No Shirt, No Service.
Tiny Bubbles in the Wine. Sweet Beulah Land. Gone Fishing.

Any make-up exam will be significantly harder
than the one you should have been there for in the first place.

Blood on the Saddle. Money in the Bank. A Few Pickles Shy of a Barrel.
I Don't Know Art, But I Know What I Like.

Let's not mistake whatever isn't Hell for part of Heaven.

iii. Last Name Last

The world's last name is whatever we come up with when we leave it, ready
or not, even if no one else in the room can hear us—
if there is a room, if anybody else is hanging around.
It's the last thing we have to say, even if we can't quite speak it
out loud. It can't be as familiar as the world we were so sure of
having all the time in. The last name of the world is likely
something dusky, if not altogether dark. The last name of the world assuredly
is nothing that will have even once occurred to us before.
The last name of the world distinguishes it, finally,
as still the only place that can sustain our fragile selves
among so many scorched or frozen, far less habitable worlds.
The last name of the world is inescapable and, right now at least,
we can live with that—as long as we don't really know
what it means. The last name of the world will be unmistakably ours.

No More Mail from Baltimore

for David Hilton

I never saw your dying, but it came
to where you felt it right in front of you.
I'd rather give it any other name.

Come hell or heaven, dying's much the same—
it's always the last thing we're left to do.
I never saw your dying, but it came

and did its hula dance, its candle flame.
And if the Afterlife proves something new,
I know you'll work on jazzing up its name.

Down here, in the long run, we pull up lame.
The smoke of our own breath can't see us through.
I never saw your dying, but it came.

Your cancerous father lived on borrowed fame—
the hotel you swore no relation to.
It's too late now to try another name.

I'd like to say it hasn't been my aim
to write you back to life on Earth. It's true
I never saw your dying, but it came
in your last letter, signed with your good name.

So Much Gone and Going

A young star, T Tauri Component Sb, *has been gravitationally ejected from a star group in the constellation Taurus, 450 light-years from Earth. It could slow down over many years and remain within the gravitational grasp of its star family, making a wide loop and eventually heading back home. Or it may have found enough escape velocity to leave for good.*

    —AP wire story

i.

But from this distance, to my untrained naked eye, nothing
seems that astronomically out of whack. I can't see
any celestial cause for alarm.
       Just ask Eddie Ponicsan,
my third-grade classmate who ran away from home, who survived
almost two weeks in an alley behind the White Rose Diner, barely
a dozen blocks from his own front door, before finally giving in
and giving up for good his fugitive ways.
       A scary few years later
it was Jimmy Horvath running into the bad dream of his life—
grabbing a bat, chasing an armed intruder into the autumn moonlight
and never coming back.
       And I'd wake up soon enough to Debbie Fuller,
suddenly moving with her family—a totally unheard-of quantum leap
to Basking Ridge, New Jersey. Some nights I can almost make her out
in the dimming constellations of a childhood light-years away:
Old Man Cooper's Five & Dime. Her mother's ancient robin's-egg-
blue station wagon. The red-dirt playground haze of Hamilton School.

But thanks to science, I have to admit it's more likely the light
from wherever Debbie Fuller used to be—radiant, shimmering,
atmospheric—coming back the long way home to me.

ii.

There's a lot of leaving in the world—let alone
in the unsettled vastness of the universe. Greyhound busses.
Wives and boyfriends. Sailors running wild on shore. Hotel guests
and partygoers. Entire rain-forest species we've never heard of,
checking out by the hundreds. Refugees from war and love,
hands full of anything left to hold onto, on the move for days
or years, getting away with their lives.
                                              Even more or less at home,
where the roof still hasn't fallen in completely, we might finally
leave well enough alone, no matter how imperfect. Leave it be.
If there's going to be trouble in the living room again,
we could leave it, just this once, for someone else. Leave us
out of it, please. And if we end up leaving a light on
before disappearing into a night that will only get longer,
it's more a way of saying we forgot to turn it out
than anything it could possibly say about making our 40-watt stand
against the dark. As if there's really somewhere else
we have to be. As if we'll somehow know it when we get there.

And when we tell ourselves and anyone else who's listening,
looking on from an admittedly unbelievable distance,
that we won't be back, ever, or that we most certainly will—
depending on which *no* or *yes* this time is the tiny lozenge of bravado
worn down but incredibly intact on the tip of the tongue—
chances are, either way, it's a promise light-years beyond
our ability to keep it. As empty as interstellar space.

With so much gone and going, we're sure to be, sooner
or later, what's left: the stars of our own small lives.
We've slowed down through the years, inexplicably drawn again
to the gravity of so many situations we actually believed ourselves
beyond for good, to the lights we left still burning there.
It's amazing there's not a lot more burning-out in the world—
let alone in the dogged, star-studded firmament.

iii.

Because this is America, there's really StarBright, Inc.—
after paying their Galactic Finder's Fee of $99.95, you're entitled
to name, as you wish, one previously undesignated star.
Considering the magnitude of the gesture, it's usually a misguided,
romantic, or last-minute gift, a little something bound to outshine
those clunky astronomers' darlings like *Regulus* or *Betelgeuse* or *Rigel*.
StarBright's got an infinite supply of brilliant orphans waiting
for your call.
              They'll enter the name in some Giant Star Registry,
and of course there's a certificate suitable for framing, plus a guide
to finding it from anywhere, anytime, in any season's night sky.
And in the unlikely event your chosen star goes supernova
in your lifetime, you'll get a less volatile replacement absolutely free.

For all of this, there's no waiting. No laborious background checks.
Serial killers, CEOs, the kid working nights at the neighborhood 7-Eleven:
it's the great star-struck democracy of hundred-dollar bills.
And whether or not it's legal, universally recognized, or even
astronomically binding, at this rate it does seem that the sky indeed
is the limit—you could name an entirely anonymous constellation
for less than you've lost on your worst nights at the track.

But I'd go slowly if I were you. I'd point in a general, far-off way
to that upstart, so unceremoniously ejected, just now making its move.
I'd say, *That's the one I want to put my money on.* One hundred bucks
and whatever still remains of your own wavering light—no escape
velocity's worth any more than that, I'm betting. If I were you.
Maybe somewhere out there, heading into the long first turn, the former
T Tauri Component Sb—no longer saddled with that makeshift name
by astronomers, who clearly have no business naming stars—will one day
get the chance Eddie Ponicsan never had: to come from behind,
flying down the stretch, the dark horse bringing home the roses.
Or to end up in a not-too-shabby second place. Or at least to finish
in some version of the money by showing up third, anywhere in the sky.

Don't we wish. And furiously. We've had a world of practice wishing
our whole lives. By this time we can do it with our eyes closed, even
when we're otherwise exhausted, out-of-pocket, one fledgling star away
from being right back in the dark we started from.

The Flamingos Have Left the Building

Place them in garden or on lawn to beautify landscape—$2.76 per pair.
      —1957 Sears Catalogue listing for the original flamingo lawn ornament
      (Union Products, Leominster, Massachusetts)

for Becky Shaw, conservator

Just shy of fifty years since it arrived,
the classic pink flamingo's gone extinct,
done in by the rising cost of plastic
and unrelenting flood of Chinese knockoffs.

A 22-year-old Don Featherstone
designed the birds for hometown Union Products.
They flew off store shelves, landing everywhere,
and Leominster, Mass., was in the pink.

They ruled the roost of lawn-art kitsch before
the gnomes and bug-eyed frogs moved in to stay—
a nod to all those bronze and marble statues
on more expansive properties than theirs.

In those days one was never quite enough.
You paired them up or, better yet: a flock,
a sudden conflagration of bright pink
flamingos in the hottest yards around,

and next-door neighbors surely had to think,
There goes the neighborhood, or else, *We've got
to get us some of those before too long.*
But now it's too late—going, going, gone.

In pink flamingo transmigration
they left their yards for other habitats—
festooning tablecloths and dinner plates
or showing up in paint-by-number kits,

as earrings, window shades, and whirligigs,
and in disguise: sunglasses, bedroom slippers,
umbrellas, walking-sticks, and floppy hats,
then stirring cocktails, shaking salt and pepper,

or trapped inside of souvenir snow-globes
a long way from the natural Florida sun.
When a good flamingo idea goes bad,
they're accessories after the plastic fact.

My friend insists her purple house is where
she caught a poacher in her yard, pink-handed,
in floodlights she installed after she learned
new birds of Featherstone would flock no more.

Like any cause that's lost, they were absorbed
into the culture they did not bring down.
No leg to stand on now, defenseless, but
still undeniably there on Becky's lawn.

In My Dream, Coleman Hawkins

walked right up to me at the corner of West 52nd and Broadway,
and he actually said, *Do you know how to get to*
Carnegie Hall? And even in my dream I realized
he'd been dead since 1969, although I still couldn't believe it,
his not knowing Carnegie Hall was only blocks away,
so I figured he'd meant all along to be setting me up instead,
but who was I to deliver a punch line to the Hawk
himself, the royal Bean—to my ear, the unmistakable
heavyweight champion of the tenor saxophone world?
I'll blow you a real quick chorus or two
if you help me out just this one time, man—and
that's exactly what the late Coleman Hawkins did.
So, finally, I had to tell him: *Practice.* And I guess
he had to laugh: *That's really what I needed to hear.*
Then he thwacked me with his immortal horn, and I woke up
to the coolest breeze through any window, ever, my head still ringing
with every strain of his *Body and Soul.*

Goodbye to the Blockhead

*Anyone who's ever hammered a nail into his nose owes a large debt to
Melvin Burkhart.*
> —Todd Robbins, Burkhart's friend and fledgling blockhead

for Melvin B., the beloved Human Blockhead (1907–2001)

i.

He always swore that it didn't hurt—not with his boxer's nose broken
so many times and the dozen bone fragments removed from his face—
that one day he just picked up a pair of five-inch spikes and wondered
what it might take to make a name for himself, exactly, in this life.
How he did it was no secret. The trickier question *why*, he answered: *because
I can.* And for more than sixty years, he did his tough-as-nails-guy act
in front of millions, one ten-minute show at a time: from the spectacular
Ringling Brothers big top to the subterranean Times Square hipster digs
of Hubert's Museum. From the 1939 New York World's Fair (*Come See
the Face of Tomorrow!*) to Ripley's Believe It or Not Odditorium,
to the Coney Island boardwalk hubba-hubba. And in a thousand
no-name towns, along the red-dirt carnival midway of the James E. Strates
Traveling Show, where he carried on fifteen times a day. He always swore
that he hadn't lost his head. He was in it for the long haul, the never-ending
thrill of the spiel, his pilfered Borscht Belt patter: *My doctor
hit the nail on the head when he told me what I needed to keep going
was more iron.* Until every crowd came through with its collective groaning,
but never in actual pain. Until maybe they couldn't take it any longer,
laughing at last in the ridiculous face of danger.

         This blockhead business
was a cotton-candy breeze compared to the grueling diet of acts
he'd cut his carny teeth on. So farewell to the swords, farewell
to the fire, farewell to everything he'd surely swallowed for too long.
And good riddance to the Homemade Electric Chair, mercifully broken down
to its sure-fire hot-plate element. Melvin Burkhart drank his coffee strong.

ii.

And if by now you're wondering *who* could love a Blockhead so: her name is
Joyce, his wife of fifty years. In all that time, she couldn't bear
to watch him work, but she survived him. And still does. He never failed
to send his money home to her in Florida, where she tacked his corny postcards
to the walls of their trailer. Wishing he was there.

         This is a so-long
song for the Blockhead, for all his road-weary companions walking through
the valley of the sideshow of death: may they fear no mortal evil.
May they find themselves playing to crowds they never dreamed of in their lives.
But especially that man with the legendary hammer, unmistakably right up there
with John Henry and Thor, God of Thunder, and my Saturdays-forever-on-the-ladder
father—his mouth full of nails because he's got to carry them somehow
on his deliberate way to the top of his twice-mortgaged world. Because he can.
Who, one astonishing Saturday, took me to Coney Island instead:
You won't believe the Human Blockhead. But right away, I did.

iii.

         It's no secret
we crawled out headfirst into this life that sometimes can't help
driving us crazy. Maybe the trick is in holding on, doing what we can
and somehow making it look easy. If we're lucky, we find something

so genuinely simple that it won't take too much. The art is in that kind of
graceful acquiescence. Don't take just the Blockhead's stand-up word for it.
Ask the inscrutable Master of the Obvious, ask Our Lady
of the Nameless Miseries. Ask the Astounding Bundle of Nerves,
the Torturer's Apprentice, the Tedium King. Ask the Hero of a Thousand
Likely Stories, the Quivering Mass, Mr. Take-It-Out-On-Others-
Until-It-Feels-Mostly-Gone. Until the slapdash ride is suddenly
over and someone's flying through the windshield, one more hard bargain
driven into the way-too-accommodating face of God, or the face
of his fallen-star competition. Or maybe the blank face of eternity,
empty beyond expression—a vacant lot where we could have sworn
the carnival was supposed to be.
                              And that has to hurt, no matter what,
because there's such a good crowd of people still very much alive.
Way up high in nosebleed heaven, they're crying in the cheap seats
for every one of us. Sure, they're curious as hell
but not exactly dying to find out, not yet, how any part of this act
is finally done.

iv.

                    This time I really can't believe the Human Blockhead.
It hit me strangely hard, how much I can't stand
that he's gone to Blockhead dust and glory. Gone the way
of my father thirty years earlier, who was born as well
in 1907. Who took me out of his way to Coney Island
and died too soon. That still hurts where I think it shouldn't,
where part of my already fragmented self was broken further
and too much removed, and I went so long and stupid pretending otherwise
without trying nearly hard enough to let someone that far inside again,
where she'd see everything I was, how I couldn't help feeling, and she might
get down on the floor with the pieces of my life and love me for them—

a death-defying act of faith I could never manage working alone.
By now I'd gladly send a thousand postcards at once to the Other Side
if I could, if only I had a reliable address: *Never stopped*
wishing you were here. And one more, mailed home to the only woman alive
who could love such an achingly imperfect, lower-case blockhead so.

I'd like to think both of these guys would know why, for just a moment,
I'm bringing them together here: because I can. Because
they occurred to me. It's more than the surprising birth-year coincidence,
more than their abiding reverence for the marriage of hammer and nail:
they weren't afraid to go, their separate ways, for broke
into their everyday matters of life and death or a shot of the hard stuff,
love. To go against the conventional wisdom—so sure were they,
even at the end, that some things in this world will always be
more easily done than said.

The Only Time There Is

for my mother

i.

She died three weeks before Ben was born, although at least
she knew her grandson was coming, he was on his own mortal way,
and even in her going she was glad for all of us, glad
that on one of the few lucid days in her last year
she'd met my wife in person and actually remembered everything.
At the kitchen table the two of them gathered up my mother's life
in photographs—eighty-five years in a single afternoon.
They couldn't help but laugh and love each other right away
in the only time there was. And from the corner of her eye,
I think my mother must have seen her own, inexplicable son
somehow in the middle of his life, at last so undeniably
happy she could die.

ii.

                    Riding high in the grocery-store cart,
sometimes Ben would get this far-off look for a minute.
And then he'd be on his way again, unmistakably grinning
back into the thick of his otherwise-nonstop talking.
And, once, I heard it too, or thought I did: my mother's voice,
that same mild way she had in real, soft-spoken life—my mother,
who'd quietly drive all over town to save a dime on lettuce,

a quarter on juice, an entire dollar on Breyer's coffee ice cream,
my father's one sweet weakness.
                                And finally it came to me:
what better place than the frozen-foods aisle at the Safeway
to let us know what she's not missing completely.

iii.

Yesterday, when I grabbed a box of his favorite mints
while we stood in the checkout-line, Ben told me: *I bet
we could find them cheaper, Dad.* And I have to believe him
when he says he can always find out where.

All Night and Always

for Patricia

i.

If there really is a Great Beyond,
or even a Pretty Good Beyond,
you're the only person I know
I could actually spend that kind of time with
and not be sneaking a look at my watch every eon or so.

If we all return to particles of dust
or ambient light or the subatomic glory
of far-flung Alpha Centaurian star-stuff,
then I want at least some of my particles
right in the thick of your come-hither particle whirl.

If we have voices, then I can promise you
I'm home-free. I'd know your golden-tongued delivery
anywhere. Even without the benefit of ears,
I'd vibrate up and down the length
of whatever I've somehow managed to become.

And if we have any kind of explicit shape—
ethereal projections or holograms or exotic
see-through apparitions of whoever we used to be—

I'll do my best to contain my ectoplasm
until you've manifested your own ectoplasm.

ii.

If there's any Afterlife at all, who better than the once-skeptical
Houdini to say so, according to the plan worked out with his wife,
just in case, before he died: a prearranged message, to be conveyed
to his living Bess, reaching back through the complications of so much
time and space, touching on their earliest, easiest days in love—
but a message so absurd on its surface that no medium ever
would scam together those particular words out of the spiritless air.
Just because she never heard them doesn't mean Houdini wasn't
really somewhere, more desperate than usual to find at last
even one genuine clairvoyant. For all we know, he might have been
busting his metaphysical gut to answer the curtain call of a lifetime.
It doesn't mean they're not together again, traveling the boondocks
of some untold astral realm, living out of a trunk that won't ever quit.

So when I'm that far gone myself, away from you for who-knows-
how-long, as long as it isn't for good, here's what I propose.
I want you to listen hard for the phrase we fell in love with
together, right away, all night and always at the Idle Hour Lounge,
where Tiny poured you a sturdy tumbler of his sorry house wine
while passing on his down-to-earth assurance: *You get more
in a regular glass.* We thought we'd died and gone to Taproom Heaven.
But three years later, that was Tiny instead. He's still pouring,
still larger than life on the Other Side, if it's there. And maybe
he can help me get across to you, again, those words to live by.
If you hear them from either one of us, I'm telling you now
there you'll have it—absolute proof of our kind of spirit world,
forever living up to its reputation.

iii.

And if it turns out there's only the Great Right Now,
and we have no better offers, nowhere else they're waiting
just for us, you'll have to pardon me for thinking
I can live with that. Some nights with nothing but you
to hold onto, I've been eternally grateful anyway.
I've felt as if I could have lived forever, without question,
at that breathtaking latitude and longitude, right here
on Earth as it is. As surely it was always meant to be.

And when, in this version, it comes to dying, I want you there,
holding your pocket mirror up to the very end of my breathing
while I steam it silly for as long as I possibly can—
as if we're living in some never-ending nineteenth-century novel
where there's no machinery in sight that could measure
the vital signs packing every one of their impossibly small bags
or the height I'm about to fall from, once and for all,
with you still somehow on my lips, all the way down into what
I'm guessing is the not-so-perfectly accommodating ground.

The All-Dressed-Up-and-Going-Nowhere Ghosts

> *A question that ghost researchers are trying to answer: If ghosts are residual human*
> *spirit energy, why do their full-body manifestations so often include the societal*
> *convention of clothing?*
>   —from an article in *FATE Magazine*

i. The Body Electric

Because we are, oddly, in the flesh, so relentlessly electric—
full of pulses and charges and static, even the occasional spark—
and because the body is so immutably three-quarters water,
it's a wonder that a lot of us are around for as long as we are,
always pushing our luck. We're the live radio in the bathtub.

And because the body generates electromagnetic energy,
a field that must conform to the body's actual contours,
then, more days than not, that energy has to look remarkably
like us. What fervent, nineteenth-century Spiritualists insisted
on calling the *etheric body* may be more like an animated Jell-O mold
of whoever we are, corporeally speaking.

                        And when the body dies
and there's nothing else in the world we can think of, we give up
the ghost, as literally as possible. And who's to say that part of us,
suddenly left to its own otherworldly devices, isn't
exceedingly conscious, with newfangled metabolic power?

If disembodied spirits have a sense of self-control
and can rearrange their energy any way they want to,
eyewitnesses might see those dispositions as the spirits see themselves:
paler shades of human beings, maybe, but no less modest for that.
No less self-conscious than ever. And so: wearing clothes.

They've dressed for the occasion as a way of helping us, too—
we who are still living and so often seem to need it.
They're hoping to be recognized for exactly who they are this time
and that, by their clothing, we shall know them.

ii. A Less-Than-Full-Bodied Experience

Ghosts that can't quite manage human forms
don't worry about getting dressed. They do what they can
as energy less fully realized, more abstracted than defined:
a fleeting light, a vapor, a haze, an inexplicable mist
or, even more vaguely, a whisper of air, a sudden cold spot
in a room where the intangible might be absorbing heat
in an effort to energize further, to manifest itself as anything
even the slightest bit visible. And it just so happens
we've wished for that kind of viability ourselves. Whole days
and nights of trying, and we understand—a lack of attire
is the least of their problems. If you're an orb, you already know
you haven't got a thing to wear.

But still:
when researchers are ghosting at the next night's haunting grounds—
presuming ghosts will always show up better in the dark—
they should try a more sartorial approach. Along with the requisite
latest in spook-finder electronics—the magnetic-field meters,
thermal-imaging cameras, motion-sensitive digital video recorders—
they should be equipped with needle and thread, some scissors,
an infrared sewing machine. A few bolts of cloth—a nice cotton,
maybe. Material that breathes. Bring a haberdasher,
a milliner, a tailor. Show the spirits something drop-dead
gorgeous in a 42-long, in a form-fitting angora sweater,
in a snazzy snap-brim hat with a feather in the band—anything
a cut above the usual thrift-store spectral garb.
Something they might gladly consent to be seen in, now
and again, if only they can pull themselves together, somehow
try this whole new image on for size.

iii. Unfinished Business

One school of spirit-realm thought says ghosts don't see themselves
as dead. There wasn't enough time to try on that idea
and live with it, even for a day. They were taken somehow
by surprise, or else they surely would have packed a change of clothes.
They act as if they're feeling more alive than ever, flying
in the face of the incredibly long odds against their being
anything more than illustrations of our mostly wishful thinking.

When spirits linger here among us, it's likely some troubling matter
of unfinished business—apparently no small thing when you're a ghost.
Many hauntings have been known to stop completely
when someone still alive discovers what's been left behind, undone—
an unaccomplished mission no ghost can possibly see through, alone—
and manages to finish what was started another lifetime away.
In movies, it's always dramatic: finally bringing a killer to justice
or razing the houses so heedlessly built on ancient burial grounds.
In real life, it's not necessarily as noble as all that.

And it's never a porn-star ghost with unfinished business in the bedroom—
a full-body apparition that could actually be convincing.
Too often it's that monk in his trademark cowl and shapeless vestments,
or another lost Confederate soldier in faded grey, or the widow
eternally staring through her funereal veil at what passes for the world.
And plenty of children, of course, dressed in those ludicrous, impossible
eighteenth- and nineteenth-century children's clothes that make them look especially
frightening, disturbingly so much older than they ever grew to be.

———◆◆◆◆◆———

Then there's the late Uncle Bud, Conspiracy-Thinking's most dogged disciple—
not orb or intermittent light, neither completely transparent nor translucent
but rather, my as-opaque-as-ever uncle. Sometimes he's not all there,
but I can usually make out his quintessential features:
that ubiquitous overcoat and fedora, to this day amazingly intact.
He's been to the Other Side and halfway back, and if he's any more
illuminated now, he doesn't show it. And it's nothing he can say.
Clearly, he's unshrouded the mystery of a lifetime—when it comes to death,
he's in the know. And maybe he's also discovered where the rest of the bodies
are buried—and who's better off, and by how much, not knowing.

If I'm supposed to help my uncle finish what he couldn't—
expound upon his arcane findings, present his madcap theories to the world
whose deepest covert workings he made it his daily business to uncover—
I have no idea where to start. He'd always thought of himself
as a scientist of Conspiracy, working his way toward the elusive Unified
Inside-Job Theory of Everything. He's so far out of the mortal loop now,
he probably can't believe it. And since he isn't talking, who's to say,
after what he's been through lately, that things aren't somehow
different with him? Maybe now he'd concede there's a ghost of a chance
that JFK was shot by only Oswald, the United States really did land
a few men on the Moon, space aliens didn't come close to crash-landing
in the desert outside Roswell, and there has never, ever been a pill
you could put in the gas tank and get 200 miles to the miraculous gallon.
And the *They* who weren't about to let slip with any of this hush-hush news
is, in sad fact, just a lower-case *they* who really don't understand
a single whisper more than anybody else,
who couldn't cover up something even as small as a sleeping baby.

I helped Bud one other time in both our lives that I remember—1957,
when he built his homemade secret weapon, an unlikely light-beam
contraption he swore would bring down that upstart of a Russian satellite.

And if my assistance now could mean he wouldn't be coming back this way
as often or at all, then I guess I'm not about to make that happen.
I'd rather not live in any world unhaunted by his cockeyed likes.
It would be a more orderly and ordinary world—the one Bud secretly feared
and never admitted: where people wake up and get dressed for another day
of business as usual. And my Uncle Bud, triumphant in defiance,
with none of that kind of clothing to his honorable name.

iv. To Each Ghost, Its Own Style

If I have anything at all to say about it
when I get my ghostly marching orders, I'll be the one
in the Loch Ness Monster T-shirt and flying saucer baseball cap,
making my spirited rounds of the places I've haunted
all my life: junk shops, flea markets, second-hand bookstores,
the back booth at White Castle. Maybe even the long-gone
Idle Hour Lounge, which so deserves its rematerialization
out of the ether every no-frills tavern eventually is doomed to:
like some crazy taproom version of the accursed *Flying Dutchman*,
but on calmer, neighborhood seas. With massive Larry at the helm
as always, and nothing but blessings in the air.

                                                I'll be a regular
swell of a ghost—something, finally, for anyone to believe in
absolutely. I'll show up in photographs as substantially more
than a reflection or smudge on the lens. I'll stick around
for more than a few seconds at a time. I'll do the phantom
bells and whistles. I'll be so outgoing, no one would ever guess
it was me, if not for my wardrobe—surely a dead giveaway.
And as for the Bigfoot slippers I've been forever hunting,
so I can pad around, perfectly quiet, when I want to:
I'll work on making those myself through my sheer, electromagnetic will.

v. For Every Ghost, a Solid Reason Why

Because there's a chill in the air like you wouldn't believe
between here and there—between this life and, with any luck,
the next one. And given what some people swear they've seen,
it might take awhile to get there, even as our mostly energetic selves.
Dressed in something that still fits, that's warm enough this time
so we won't catch our death all over again.

Untold Days on Earth

Although the space program was begat by the Cold War, the lunar landings still looked like such a crazy Sixties thing. . . . No Merry Prankster or acid-popping mystic ever did anything freakier than this, and yet the ambiguities of the enterprise seemed endless.
        —Andrew Smith, *Moondust*

Uncle Bud, Unshaken in the Wake of *Sputnik:* October 1957

i.

Maybe because they were strangely so much alike: 180 pounds
and transmitting essentially meaningless signals from their distance—
although *Sputnik*, with its intermittent beeping, was moving undeniably
faster than my uncle, orbiting the Earth every hour-and-a-half.
It took Bud that long just to wake up, make coffee, and scramble his eggs
before heading into another day full of his unfinished, get-rich-quick
inventions, muttering to himself on his unhurried way to anywhere.
Overnight, the Russians had clearly taken most of the world by surprise,
and what, exactly, was that satellite supposed to be doing up there, anyway?
No one ever really knew what Uncle Bud was up to, either,
clanking and banging through so many impossible nights in his workshed,
but they weren't about to lose any real sleep over him.

ii.

The only reason for the beeping: a one-volt-battery-powered radio transmitter
so *Sputnik* could be tracked over those three weeks before it fell
silent. It stayed in orbit another seventy days, visible to anyone looking up
just beyond the familiar horizon. And Uncle Bud couldn't help but look
quietly upon it, every chance he got. He saw it as someone's personal triumph,
no matter how small—old-fashioned know-how flying high, before the inevitable
crash-and-burn.

Half a world away, Little Richard saw it too,
during an outdoor concert in Australia, and took it somehow as a sign
more divine than ingeniously human. Immediately, he walked off the stage,
renounced rock 'n' roll, and for a while fell into his own good-golly
brand of evangelism. But Uncle Bud was saying to hell with rock 'n' roll
long before *Sputnik* was even a gleam in Little Richard's wide eyes.

iii.

And while the Cold War was taken to new, out-of-this-world heights, the fear
was still down-to-earth. The country that had launched this harmless beach ball
of a satellite surely wasn't doing it for fun, could just as easily
target anywhere on the planet with a guided nuclear warhead. And this
was only a guess: that would be us. And so a suddenly white-knuckled USA
got cracking. Thanks to those no-goodnik Russians, I'd soon be weighed down
with more grade-school science and arithmetic than I'd ever counted on,
now that we had serious catching-up to do—even if no one could touch us
when it came to engineering the coolest automotive tail fins in the world.

iv.

On the same day that *Sputnik* was fired into orbit—the first in an upcoming
flurry of launches we insisted, for a while, on calling *space-shots*—
Jimmy Hoffa was elected Teamsters president. He stayed aloft for years
before disappearing into the vastness of some different space altogether.
Leave It to Beaver was just getting off the television ground that night.
And the Yankees, the goddamn Yankees, were back again in the World Series,
where it would be up to Braves pitcher Lew Burdette, spitball or not,
to shut them down and finally out.
                          In the year of the ill-fated Edsel,
which went absolutely nowhere, in the year of the worst flu outbreak
since the end of World War I, Americans were also coming down all over

with acute *Sputnik*-itis—an unhealthy obsession with Russia's eye-opener.
Headlines like RED MOON OVER AMERICA had them knocking back their share
of Sputnik Cocktails: two parts vodka, one part sour grapes.
They'd lighten up later with Sputnik lamps, Sputnik hairdos,
Sputnik shish kebob. They'd come to say *going Sputnik* for anything
that seemed even the least bit way out there, like Uncle Bud himself,
or like those newly christened *beatniks* that Bud had no time for, either.
But first it was the night-sweats, weakness, a national case
of the willies. Report after unconfirmed report had *Sputnik* setting off
thousands of those new electric garage-door openers all across the country.

V.

Twelve years later, America would finally put its foot down,
beating the Russians to the Moon. Bud would find it tough to believe
anyone was truly on the Moon and not a top-secret movie set hidden away
in Arizona or somewhere else he'd never been. My Uncle Bud—
always one small step or two ahead of his conspiratorial time.
Either way, it was hard to imagine in 1957—not even that much cold comfort
in the shadow of *Sputnik* on those crisp October nights, a long way from any
Sea of Tranquillity, from Armstrong and Aldrin and especially that third guy,
just along for the high-powered ride. The one who'd get stuck with
staying behind, locked into his solitary lunar orbit, no doubt cursing
his short-straw luck—forever miles away from any real historic action.
Of everything NASA would try to sell him, that much, at least, Bud would buy.

vi.

The only beeping I heard was the horn of Bud's worn-out Buick.
From my bedroom window I could see him again, painfully visible
to the naked eye, straining under the weight of whatever he was lifting
this time out of the trunk: a patchwork masterpiece of metal, bulbs, and wires

he began to assemble in the moonlit driveway—two parts Buck Rogers
and one part Sears, Roebuck—taking me into his ridiculous confidence again
because I was the only one in the family who believed in him, or at least
believed in the idea of him: *I've been working on something
that can bring it crashing down.* Uncle Bud had thought it over
and decided, on behalf of the greater good, there was nothing else to be done.
And so there we were, mostly in the dark, aiming his latest contraption
into space, whatever it was, both of us hunkering down in our Cold War
rosebushes bunker, waiting for anything small and brilliant to flash by
over our heads, for the telltale garage door to open for no apparent reason.
But he would know better—and me too, just then, for knowing him.

                                                        And when
the motorized garage door actually lifted, we still could hardly believe it:
my mother standing at the switch, awakened from a fitful sleep, not quite
dreaming what was going down that night, right there in her own
American backyard. My uncle and I were no rocket scientists, but
we had a feeling—*Sputnik* or no *Sputnik*—there was going to be trouble
if she spotted us in the bushes among her beloved American Beauties, or what
was left of them that late in the year. Those reds and purples: the only
true colors of blood and bruise—as if all the radiant pain of being alive
had come together in a single tight bud, making ready to blossom
into one last, inexplicably joyful noise.

Home Movies of the Space Race

I believe that this nation should commit itself to achieving the goal, before
this decade is out, of landing a man on the Moon and returning him safely
to the Earth.

           —JFK, 1961 address to Congress

i. A Little Respect

At Hamilton Elementary we watched every *Mercury* launch
between the Pledge of Allegiance and our ration of morning milk
on the battered TV that janitor Geiss always lugged into our room,
trailing a whiff of the Lucky Strikes that somehow kept him going
in the humble boiler-room office he liked to call his very own
Mission Control.

           The entire class would count down together
until the launch-tower fell away, the rocket-booster fuel igniting
with the kind of brilliant firepower that in those days never failed
to lift our skittish hearts into our throats. We were suckers
for anything astronautical—the suits, the helmets, the very idea
of leaving the outmoded Earth behind us for a while. We'd come
to live for the chance of escaping the pull of preadolescent gravity.

So who among us would have believed we'd peter out so quickly,
even before *Apollo*? We ho-hummed our way through most of *Gemini*,
although Ed White's tethered space walk brought us briefly back.
The way he floated outside that capsule, doing exactly what,
we weren't sure, led Sci-Fi Rosenberg to say maybe he'd grow up
to be the first Jew on Mars. Benny the Ball kept asking when

do Current Events become History, and then would there be a test?
I made a brazen grab for Debbie Fuller's hand. I really didn't know
what I was doing either, but I might have been floating too,
until Mr. Geiss told us all to knock off the funny stuff, to show
a little respect—as if White could possibly look down right at us
and refuse to clamber back inside until he had our full attention.
Geiss was a Big-Picture guy: he saw the whole country being tested,
and this was the kind of lapse in judgment we simply couldn't afford
if we were going to beat those single-minded Russians to the Moon.

ii. My Father Was a Guy Grissom Man

and he couldn't believe John Glenn was the astronaut
who'd sent America into orbit in his *Friendship 7*. My father, still
shaking his head long after splashdown: *What kind of soft-boiled name
is* Friendship 7, *anyway?* Even though Glenn was a decorated Marine,
he was far too apple-pie-goody for my father—and for Gus Grissom, too,
from what my father had gathered. *It really should have been Gus,*
he insisted—5′6″ and 160 pounds of scrappy fighter-pilot power.
He's a brick torn out of a wall—absolutely the highest praise
my father could put into words.
                  And in the burgeoning wild
and wooly 1960s, my father admired Grissom's stubborn crew cut
and his verbal reticence, a far cry from Glenn's launching into
those buoyant, freckle-faced answers to every reporter's question,
no matter how insipid. My father liked how Grissom spent his Sundays
drag-racing at the beach, while Glenn, for God's sake, went mostly
smiling and waving into church. My father believed utterly in Grissom:

Gus, who grudgingly accepted his lot as the second man shot into space,
a fifteen-minute suborbital lob in *Liberty Bell 7—because freedom's
important to a guy like Gus.* When the hatch blew open prematurely,
Liberty Bell went down for the count, and Grissom nearly drowned.
Gus, who almost single-handedly designed the two-man *Gemini* craft
and flew its inaugural mission, naming his capsule the *Molly Brown—*
after the Unsinkable One then playing to packed Broadway houses.
Gus, who smuggled onboard a Woolfie's Deli corned beef sandwich,
wreaking his unabashedly meaty havoc with NASA protocol.
My father loved that story the most—when it came to sandwiches, he was
a corned beef man all the way. Glenn was strictly baloney-and-cheese.
Gus, who was promised the first *Apollo* mission too, but who wanted more
than anyone alive to be that first man with his boot-sole on the Moon.

For his birthday—January 27, 1967—my father got a necktie
and the news he couldn't swap for something better: Florida,
fire, *Apollo 1*. Rookie Roger Chaffee, space-walker Ed White, and
hardest of all for my father to swallow, Virgil (Gus) Grissom—
killed where they sat, Earthbound, Pad 34, during a routine
systems-check and simulated countdown gone awfully wrong.
NASA needed them inside to help work out the glitches
a pissed-off Grissom had complained about for weeks: bad connections,
crossed wires, erratic signals—way too much not up to speed.
He'd hung an enormous Texas lemon in the window the day before.

And on my father's birthday, Grissom was shouting into his headset
for the computer jockeys in the blockhouse down the road: *I can't hear
a thing you're saying. How the hell are we going to get to the Moon
if we can't talk between two or three buildings?* But at 6:31 p.m.
the Moon had to be the farthest thing from their minds—*We've got fire
in the cockpit*—and in a flash, it was completely out of the question.
Under the sudden, suffocating pressure, there was no escaping
the fact of that difficult *Apollo* hatch. Its inward-opening design
looked so good on paper: an airtight seal like no other before
as precaution on a mission like no other before—a little something
to make extra sure the *outer* stays in *outer space* where it belongs.

And though I'm sure he meant no disrespect to White and Chaffee,
my father started breathing again: *It shouldn't have been Gus.*
Later, my uncle would say it was no accident—who knew
how long that pain-in-the-ass, perfectionist Grissom
might have kept the entire *Apollo* program from getting off the ground?
And the country didn't have that kind of time to lose.
My father never went quite that far, but he was furious at NASA,
at spectral JFK, and he couldn't help it, furious at the very idea
of God: *It shouldn't have been Gus.*

And, young as I was, I could tell
I'd have to put my own heart back into the Space Race. I'd have to take
my father's place and, somehow, Grissom's too, because they'd both faded
so fast into the night, and we weren't about to get anywhere like that.
It was up to me to fly in the face of my father's disenchantment,
even over Grissom's dead body—if that's how it had to be—
because the end of the decade would be here soon enough, and now,
more than ever, we couldn't be late for the Moon.

iii. What Some of Us Did on Our Summer Vacation: Tranquillity Base, July 20, 1969

On the hottest day of the summer, my father and I made it back
from our own Sea of Anti-Tranquillity—a jam-packed Sunday
at the Jersey shore: on the sand and in the surf, but mostly
up and down the boardwalk, full of salt-water taffy and too much
Tilt-A-Whirl. The weight-guesser nailed my father's 160 pounds
exactly, which somehow amazed him more than any luxurious fortune
Madam Starlight gladly would have told him for the same one-dollar bill.
And for the first time ever, I was the one who'd wanted to get going.
I needed to be home, sweating it out in front of the TV
with Walter Cronkite. With the unflappable voice of Houston's Mission Control.
With solitary Michael Collins, dutifully flying rings around the Moon
while Armstrong and Aldrin headed off to finish the last few miles
of the Space Race that was, mercifully, all but over.

Those hours that the two of them just sat there in the dark without moving
began to feel more like days. Everyone seemed to be waiting for the word
from somebody else, so my impatient father finally said: *Get going,*
folks, why don't you? He didn't have all night. And remarkably, barely
fifteen minutes later, they actually went—climbing down, stepping out,
then leaping into what was passing for history.

                                        It wasn't much longer
until he'd seen enough of guys named Neil and Buzz on the Moon,
and he was going to bed. My sunburned, windblown father—climbing the stairs,
minutes from his own soft landing—was suitably unimpressed.
He'd upgraded to a TV built for color, and now what did he get from the Moon
but some lousy black-and-white pictures? What was the Moon, anyway,
to him, when you got right down to it? He still had to show up
for work in the morning where, without fail, the day would weigh on him
exactly the same as so many untold days on Earth already had—and no way

could he ever find it in himself to lighten up, give in to being lifted,
even for a fleeting lunar moment, in thin air.

And while Nixon made his grandstanding long-distance call to the Moon,
Uncle Bud rang in with his own historic call to my mother, holed up
in her kitchen—perhaps the only person at home in America
who hadn't seen even a minute of the lunar goings-on: *Hey, if you think*
those guys are really up there, think again. This, from the man
who'd tried, twelve years earlier, to bring down the Russian *Sputnik*
with the newest of his wing-nut inventions. But, as they used to say
in my family, *that's another Uncle Buddha story* altogether, from before
he'd trained his ever-vigilant eye on the Moon.

My mother poured herself
more coffee and allowed for the smallest stirring of cheer. She wasn't nearly
ready for the Moon. Her twentieth century had been piling up so fast:
one day she's the Junior Jacks Champion of South Denver, stepping out of
the family Model T and into 1918's bad-dream flu epidemic. She wakes up,
somehow a Cold War grandmother, still trying to catch her breath in a world
of Boeing 727s, penicillin, power steering, and me—her youngest child
so at home in the dizzying 1960s, it's not funny. The last thing she needed
was outer space—although could someone please tell her whatever happened
to that friendly John Glenn, anyway?

She trusted me with her resignation:
Uncle Bud just called to say this isn't really happening, so I'm afraid
it probably is. Still, she had to give it to him—always the visionary
in his own way. Bud had it down to a shaky science, this genius
for ideas no one else had thought of yet. He couldn't help himself—
he'd managed a career of his preoccupations by making every one of them
work for him. And he couldn't do anything else to save his life.

iv. The Moon's Too Full for My Mother: July 20, 1969

I can't believe they're up there right now, even as we speak,
fooling around with the Moon.

The way she saw it, this was going much too far—they were acting
way too high and mighty. Out of love, God had given us
this bountiful planet, and who were we to think ourselves better
than the preordained likes of that? She could feel it
in her devoted bones—God, no doubt, getting worked up again,
about to go into another Old Testament lather—and soon
we'd all be bound to feel the repercussions somewhere:
in the weather, the murder rate, the madhouse, or worse—
at the Saturday bingo tables in suddenly high-tide Asbury Park.

But from where I sat, enveloped in the Motorola's pale
illumination, the only light in our living room, God was nowhere
in the grainy picture. He'd been resting for thousands of years
on His thinning Creation laurels. I believed more in Robert Goddard,
who in his wisdom had given us the modern age of rocketry.
I believed in the dapper von Braun and his whiz-bang firepower,
smuggled out of the brokered ruins of Nazi rocket science
and thoroughly retooled as our very own demanding father of *Apollo*.

When I finally said I couldn't believe they were up there either,
it was painfully obvious: I could hardly contain myself. I tried
telling my mother they'd gone the extra 240,000 miles for everyone,
they'd soon be leaving that very message behind in the lunar dust:

WE CAME IN PEACE FOR ALL MANKIND. But even as we spoke,
my mother closed her eyes and said please count her out.
She wasn't there yet, where I so clearly was—excited, lightheaded,
lifting off farther into my wide-open, untold future.

On the sofa my unrepentant, down-to-earth mother—a lifelong
student of gravity—was on a mission, too: worrying on our behalf.
And she could use a little peace down here. She wanted no part of
this new Moon. Already she was dreaming up again the only one
she needed—untainted, untrammeled, so full of only itself.
Usually she could see that much without leaving her own backyard.
But hours later when she woke up in the dark and walked outside,
she found herself looking into a sky so unbelievably
thick with clouds that—although she tried for all the world,
so help her—she couldn't see a blessed, goddamn thing.

Not Exactly Rocket Science

The LAPD is investigating a complaint that retired astronaut Buzz Aldrin punched gadfly filmmaker Bart Sibrel in the face after being asked to swear on a Bible that he had, in fact, been to the Moon. A cameraman with Sibrel captured most of the sidewalk altercation.

        —ABC News story

i.

And that he wouldn't swear—or couldn't, for those who insist
on reading so far into something that they fall out the other side—
is the kind of proof the We-Never-Went-to-the-Moon crowd can't get
nearly enough of. For years their hopes have been riding on
those glaringly obvious pictures, the whole world finally seeing things
their way: the *Apollo* missions were accomplished as planned
on a soundstage in Out-of-the-Way, Arizona. Or maybe New Mexico.

But it turns out there were a few unfortunate complications.
Notice the flag that ripples in a breeze where there's no atmosphere.
The telltale casting of shadows and light—so many and too much,
a geometry of the impossible. Even the way the dust rises
and falls too fast is a sign of the wrong kind of gravity at work.
And no stars appear in this improvised sky, although the astronauts
can't stop looking up and talking about them. Perhaps the fault
is not in the set-designer's stars, but in the strangely uncorrected
shooting script itself. Meanwhile, a preposterous empty bottle suddenly
rolls across the lunar floor in the raw-feed transmissions beamed into

Australian TVs before anyone with NASA had time to pick it up
and go ballistic. In a Houston minute, that was edited out of the mix.

And undoubtedly by now, a whole lot of people are thinking
it would be so much easier just to go, unmistakably, to the Moon.

ii.

Aldrin's in town to talk about his experience on the Moon. Apparently
he was dogged all day, poked and prodded with a Bible—
not the first time in history someone's been on that kind of mission.
Sibrel's in the audience, calling him a liar, a coward,
a thief for taking money to speak on a subject he knows nothing about—
not even close to the first time that's been perpetrated, either:

in *A Funny Thing Happened on the Way to the Moon*—"Exposing
the Hoaxed Moon Landing!"—Sibrel himself swears we're about to see
archival NASA footage proving the crew of Apollo 11 *never left Earth orbit
but placed a color transparency of a smaller Earth in their window,
then filmed it to simulate an actual journey to the Moon!*
                                              Not exactly
rocket science, but still: how could something that ingenious possibly
not fly? When I was ten and armed with my newfangled Polaroid Swinger,
I shot a dead bee through the windshield of my father's Chevrolet.
A minute later, it was a flying saucer buzzing the skies over Newark,
and thank God no one cared enough, in fact, to pull a Bible on me.

iii.

I've studied the purported L.A. video. I've seen the afternoon sun
bearing down on them both, and their shadows never once fail
to appear in all the right places. Sadly, it's really Los Angeles.

I can't believe Aldrin's been reduced to selling the same old
story in the City of Angels—how could he not, eventually,
lose his cool? And there I was, cheering him on.
How could his hair not get mussed up in the hot-air breeziness
of a place with so little atmosphere, it might as well be the Moon?

But we have a larger problem: Sibrel says he was *struck*
so hard that he *actually saw stars*—yet they're nowhere to be seen.
I've looked for them every time, and I'm afraid it only gets worse.
I've watched Aldrin throw that punch again and again. I've tried
slowing it down and speeding it up, turning it into one blurred
flurry of punches. I've examined the footage frame by frame,
and I'll swear: that punch never really landed. Think flying saucers
over New Jersey, not Zapruder filming in Dallas. Think Cassius Clay
in Lewiston, Maine, and Liston sprawled flat on the canvas,
but without their subsequent payday after the cheering stopped.
No wonder all charges were quietly dismissed by the end of the week,
although Mr. Funny-Thing-Happened still swears to the staggering pain
of knowing why the astronaut got off easy—the LAPD's unshakable,
wide-eyed faith in Aldrin's story: he'd been on the goddamn Moon.

And now I finally have to give it, just a little, to Sibrel.
I'd made a hero out of Buzz for something that, in fact, he didn't do.
Although he'd meant to. Although he'd honestly tried.
I should have known the first time I saw it on the TV news—
that bottle of Evian he was holding in his powerful left hand.
And he wasn't about to drop it. It wasn't about to go rolling.
So he took this sorry-looking right-handed swing
and missed—right there in Los Angeles, for everyone to see
only what they so much wanted to see. A long way from Tranquillity
and those days when he felt honored to be playing such a part in
some unbelievable history in the making.

The Lunar Sympathizers

In my opinion, lunar sympathy's a fact. It's huge. And do you know what they teach school kids instead? That we brought 842 pounds of Moon rocks back to Earth.

—manager, Ethereal Valley Café and Research Center

i.

This long-standing notion has nothing to do with taking pity on the Moon,
nor does the Moon itself commiserate, exactly, with the sorry likes of us.
Believers take it to mean that moonlight never fails to deliver
some cosmic dispensation—a portion of luck, more or less, depending
on what antic phase the Moon's going through that night. Historically,
the idea's always had legs, although it's never been attractive science.
Call it one of those *as above, so below* axioms of magical thinking,
but without the annoying arithmetic that astrologers seem to insist on.

Greco-Roman heavyweights talked up this influential Moon:
Hesiod and Horace—poets, to be sure—but also Pliny the Elder,
who'd been around the block. And even Old Man Aristotle sometimes
lost himself in lunar thought until he got so moonlight-hearted
that he was scarcely more than a shadow of his level-headed self
somewhere on the moonlit ground below.

So if living things truly do flourish in the light of a waxing Moon,
then surely there's no more fortuitous time for planting the fields,
making wine, fatting cattle, or talking a shy, loving partner in bed

through more of the 101 known positions than anybody's ever assumed
in a single night. Until it's hard to say whose radiant skin is whose.

When the Moon is on the wane, however, save what little strength is left
to harvest, to dry out, to cure what needs curing. These are not the days
to make anything but suddenly the quietest love in the world.

And the less said about the overblown full Moon, the better.
Although some still cling to an ancient belief that the Moon doesn't get
more benevolent than this, that's far from the current consensus.
Go ahead and ask the cops and paramedics, the nightshift ER nurses,
the circuit-court judge the next morning. Ask the woman in your life,
if you have one. Or the cashier at Safeway, if you must.
Yes, the full Moon made Lon Chaney famous overnight, but
that's what made him unbankable in any other cinematic light.

The new Moon might as well be no Moon at all: next-to-invisible,
not quite coming or going, it doesn't have the faintest clue
to offer in the way of either blessing or misfortune.
Those dark days and nights we're on our own, armed with nothing but
the only luck we've known from birth. And there's not much else
really to do but wait for whatever we still could have coming,
for all the good that waiting's done so far. Especially
for anyone whose luck it was to be born in the first place
under this same empty Moon. Which might as well be no luck,
not even tough luck, at all.

ii.

As long as we remember that, strictly on the level
of particle and wave, the Moon's unloading only borrowed light.
It has none of its own to shed on our decidedly mundane proceedings.

The Sun's behind this somewhere, as usual, determined to keep us going
any way it can—although some small measure of that light was actually
ours on Earth to start with, and it's only a matter of time and space
before it comes back to us: we'll put our waning faith in anything
that makes us feel just a little bigger, better than we are.

Because no matter how unlikely, we'd love nothing more
than to see some change in even the smallest part of ourselves,
a few molecules positively preening, rearranging themselves in the mirror
of the Moon's unabashed transformation. We want back that prehistoric
dimly imagined connection, wishing at very least
for a phantom leg to stand on. And we can't believe it isn't there,
even though the Moon's regeneration every month is not the magic
it used to be mistaken for. What occurs instead like celestial clockwork
is no less astronomical for that. And by asking at the same time for
so much and not nearly enough, we keep the Moon open for business.

iii.

To acquire the power of casting spells, the Chukchee shamans of Siberia
strip naked and call on the waxing Moon for their complete illumination.
And don't take this as a slam against the shamans of Siberia, but
if we have to consider those who've shed their clothing in the moonlight,
let's look instead at the women of Naples, Italy tonight. For generations
they've walked out onto balconies, fire escapes, and rooftops—
every one of them, as tradition calls for, naked and alone,
arms raised in as obvious a gesture as possible: petitioning
the Moon. Because nudity is otherwise so easily misunderstood
whenever we happen upon it.

Just look at the heavenly light
on this woman's undaunted skin, on that woman's long black hair.

And now all the women are lowering their heads, imploring, wooing
the Moon in what's surely a whisper. They have no desire, not yet
at least, to get anyone's unsolicited, lascivious attention,
but they're more afraid by far of making a mistake, however small,
in what they're about to do. In which case the whole night
will come to nothing. They're taking their lives in their hands again.
They're cupping their breasts and chanting, nine times: *Santa Luna,
Santa Stella, fammi crescere questa mammella* (*Holy Moon,
Holy Star, make this breast grow for me*).
                                        All the wind's gone out of
another long day's sails. The laundry's still hanging wet on the line.
The calamari aroma lingers in every ink-dark apartment in the city.

Santa Luna, Santa Stella: this poem may know those words, but I promise
it's not nearly as high-minded as all that. And there'll be no gratuitous
poetical waxing in its future—not when the fathers of Naples can't help
but worry in their sleep. Not when the husbands are waiting for answers
to prayers they thought they'd outgrown. And certainly not when
teenage boys, still young enough to like their chances in the street,
are moving into position, closer than ever to a hell of a miracle already
taking shape, as such things often do, still one too many stories away.

Tonight's full of people who can't believe their extraordinary luck,
no matter how this finally turns out, no matter what they end up feeling
tomorrow, when the Sun's nothing shy of its naturally brilliant self
bringing them mostly back to their senses with direct, unmitigated light.
Until they can barely remember just what they were thinking,
the Moon and everything they stayed awake for, much too late, again.

A Brief History of the Moon in Twentieth-Century Song, and Then Some

i. Mostly Wishful Thinking

The Moon has shown up more often in songs
than any other indexable noun, except for the requisite abstractions
of loneliness and love. And, okay—maybe just a few
basic elementals: fire, snow, and rain. And there for an inexplicable
1970s while: big rigs.

But my long-haul money—a flagrant abstraction—
is still on the Moon. Not that it hasn't been abstracted too, and yet
it literally keeps coming back for more, even after everything
we've put it through. It's almost always hanging around,
giving us something solid to look for in the night
instead of our own pale faces in the steamed-up bathroom mirror.
Its virtues are anything but unsung: *It's Only a Paper . . . Shine On . . .*
By the Light of . . . Old Devil . . . How High . . . and my favorite, the doo-woppy
Blue (Blue, Blue, Blue): it sees us standing alone. It knows
just what we are there for.

Songwise, the Moon inspires so many
styles of wishful thinking. Bart Howard wrote the once-inescapable
Fly Me to the Moon but, for the record, he never actually got to go.
Nor did Sinatra, Julie London, Peggy Lee. Not any of a thousand
low-rent lounge singers, either. *In other words, please be true.*
But it wasn't about to happen. It was an idea whose sheer giddiness
ran out of gas every time after only a couple of wispy verses.

In third grade, dizzy with John Glenn's ride in *Friendship 7*,
we juiced up the lyrics for our thrown-together class-play tribute:

> *Fly me to the Moon*
> *and let me look at all the stars.*
> *If you show us your planet,*
> *we will gladly show you ours.*
> *Our rocket's on the launching pad,*
> *and we would be only too glad*
> *to learn about your atmosphere, your color, and your size*
> *if to the Moon you'll let us fly.*

It didn't scan, but we tried to make it swing. Glenn himself
was never more than a hundred miles from Earth, so we decided
to go way over his head, appealing directly to those extraterrestrials
with a weakness for grade-school show tunes.

It turns out
there was no extraordinary field trip in our future.

———◆▸◀◆———

When Jonathan King recorded his pop-Existentialist anthem,
with its *streets full of people / all alone* and those meant-to-be
heartbreaking *arms that can only / lift a spoon*, he sorely needed
to believe that *Everyone's Gone to the Moon*. Maybe he wasn't exactly
shaving with Occam's Razor. But a few years later, when Nina Simone
whispered the very same thing into my high-school-sophomore ear,
for those three minutes, anyway, there could be no doubt about it.

———◆▸◀◆———

So how about some music, finally, where the Moon is truly
the Moon, and not just an image someone's desperate to dust off
until there's at least a little shine, rhetorically speaking?
Czech composer Leos Janacek's 1920 opera gets us slightly closer.
In *The Excursions of Mr. Broucek*, an ordinary citizen of Prague
boozily wafts himself up to the Moon and there encounters
creatures from his worst nightmare: the artistic and intellectual

avant-garde. He's wooed by Etherea, a delicate butterfly-being
who beseeches him to dine with her on the perfume of exotic flowers,
but Mr. Broucek can't help asking for sauerkraut and pork instead.
And just when he's thinking it can't possibly get any worse,
here comes the onslaught recitation of high-flown poetry. It's proto-
Open-Mike-Night on the Moon, and this opera's not even half-over.

ii. And Then Some

Musically speaking, when it comes to the Moon, no one's gone any farther than Lucia Pamela. Her album *Into Outer Space* didn't just take up the subject—it was also, she insisted, recorded right there on the lunar premises when she was sixty-five. Issued in 1969 by Gulfstream Records of Hollywood, Florida, and quickly slipping into the swollen river of thrift-store vinyl, the record proves nonetheless that the woman once billed as The Queen of the Squeezebox in her vaudeville days with the Ziegfeld Follies decidedly set foot on the Moon at least a year before the *Apollo 11* boys. And much more gleefully, too:

> (*Let's take a walk on the Moon—c'mon, c'mon, c'mon!*)

> *Every time I take a trip,*
> *I'm sure to meet my friends.*
> *From the sky, they fly high—*
> *this is* Hello *from them:*
> *Moo-moo-moo-moo moo-moo-moo moo-moo moo!*
> *As I was walking on the Moon,*
> *I met a little cow-ow-ow,*
> *and that's what she said to me.*

Her baker's-dozen song cycle, complete with rhapsodic stage directions, makes for a musical meteor show of whacked-out cabaret rock, heavy on the echo and reverb the Moon's so noted for. Pamela belts out her otherworldly travelogue as she happens upon a further menagerie of animals, an entire Indian village—*Who knows how they got there!*—and the practically unheard-of gooney-goon. Amid the astronomical racket of piano, accordion, clarinet, and kitchen-sink percussion, she hollers and squeals her dotty-children's-storybook lyrics without the smallest measure of irony or self-consciousness:

> (*We're gonna do a dance and a song!*)

When I say flip, *you flip.*
When I say flop, *you flop.*
When I say fly, *we'll ALL fly!*
Up to outer space we'll go
where the winds so softly blow
through the clouds hangin' low.
Touchin' the stars, Jupiter and Mars,
doin' the flip, flop, fly.
No more taxes, no more bills—
just doin' the flip, flop, fly.
Then we'll fly to the Moon—whee!—
doin' the flip, flop, fly—oh yeah!—
doin' the flip, flop, fly!

Years later, when an intrepid Fresno disc jockey tracked her down at a local church-sponsored Bingo Night: *In real life, I don't sound like I do on the record. The air's different up there, you know.*

And there is no denying that *Into Outer Space* partakes of another atmosphere altogether. It's the first inadvertent concept album in recorded history.

———◆→◇←◆———

She was born in St. Louis on the opening day of the 1904 Exposition. Twenty-two years later she was voted Miss St. Louis herself, but to her that was nothing compared to the award she received at the age of thirty-four: Best-Decorated Bicycle in the City.

She toured with one of the country's first all-girl bands, Lucia Pamela and the Musical Pirates, until hardships brought on by World War II broke up the swing-time ensemble. Subsequently, she recruited her daughter for the other half of a maybe-more-affordable duo. At Lucia's insistence, they were known as the Pamela Sisters.

I knew I couldn't help growing old, but I think I figured out a few ways around this business of growing up. *And I never settled down—not once.*

After the war she settled, if not quite down, in Fresno. She played Mother Goose, greeting visitors to Storyland, the no-frills local amusement park. She also hosted two radio shows: *The Encouragement Hour*, featuring her relentless version of the positive-thinking craze, and *Gal About Town*, her on-air society column. But mostly people knew her as the kindly eccentric lady in the lipstick-pink Cadillac.

She was cited by *Ripley's Believe It or Not* for memorizing more than ten thousand songs. And that's not even counting her own.

Her life was one enormous instrument for joy. From the moment she first held it in her youthful hands, she knew she could never stop playing.

———•◆◆•———

(*I see people! Must be the Moon People!*)

> *Eenie, meenie, miney, mo—*
> *Moontown's the place to go.*
> *Whether it's hot or whether it's cold,*
> *the weather on the Moon is the best, I'm told.*
> *On the highways and biways and valleys, it's true,*
> *there's no finer people than the Moon People, to you.*

The way she tells it, her trip to the Moon was undoubtedly the highlight of her ninety-eight years on Earth. She made a stop on Venus too, but found the recording facilities a whole lot less to her liking.

In her 1976 self-published coloring book, she further describes what she found on the Moon. It features a dog in a space-suit, smoking a cigarette—*That was actually a Moonman dressed as a dog*—and provides a glimpse of Nutland Village, populated by the likes of Messrs. Walnut, Filbert, Cashew, and Pecan, who spoke the common language of Almond—*They reminded me of the nuts I'd grown to love in Fresno!*

The prizes for her International Coloring Competition were never awarded, as no deadline had ever been announced—*I hate it when people feel rushed.*

———◆•※•◆———

(*Can you imagine where you'll be in the year 2000?*)

> *In the year 2000, just you and me—*
> *we'll walk on the Moon, just wait and see.*
> *I'll build a hut, and we'll be free—*
> *yes, free in the year 2000.*

(*I wonder where we WILL be in the year 2000. I think I'll be on the Moon.*)

She found herself living in Los Angeles instead, in a house where she kept a Christmas tree lit up all year. But until her death in 2002, she was still fundraising for her dream: an amusement park with a rocket ride that would indeed take passengers to the Moon.

And she couldn't wait to go with them.

(*I'd like to stay on the Moon, wouldn't you?*
But don't ask me why!)

And if there are people who have to believe that she came up a few miles shy of the Moon— *As long as you write this in your gooney-goon of a poem: there's never been much shy in me!*— may they realize at least Lucia Pamela still went places that most of us were thinking there's no getting to from here.

———◆•※•◆———

> *No more taxes, no more bills—*
> *just doin' the flip, flop, fly.*

iii. On Her Way to Moontown: A Son's Eulogy for Lucia Pamela (July 25, 2002)

On a summer night in San Francisco, 1943, my mother was actually
sharing a bill with the Lionel Hampton Orchestra. I was nine
and surely had better things to do, but I was in the audience anyway
when she made her enthusiastic entrance from the wings,
playing an accordion she'd covered with diamonds for the occasion.
When the floodlights hit that thing, it absolutely lit up the room.
She went into her signature back-bend, as if the weight was suddenly
too much for so small a woman. Leaning over the edge of the stage,
she ran her fingers down the keys until it sounded like the accordion
was falling and it was all she could do just to hold on.
That's exactly when the lights cut out. Everyone fell into
a disconcerting hush, and only when I couldn't help crying
did she spring up larger than life from out of that dark nowhere
back into the spotlight again, playing the rest of her song.
I heard every one of those last notes rising over the wild applause.
I saw Hampton smiling behind his vibes, flashing her the high sign:
his forefinger curled to the tip of his thumb—the O
in his gratifying O-kay!—a gesture my mother would never forget,
right up there with the Moon in her personal sky. She looked so
unbelievably radiant. And young. And just like that, I understood
what she'd always known: it was her life, to do with what she would.
Wherever it might take her. It was my mother's nutty, beautiful
life. Her life, all her life.

III

A Lifetime of Parts & Labor, Guaranteed

I heard he was up on the roof last night,
signaling with a flashlight.
And what's that tune he's always whistling?
What's he building in there?
    —Tom Waits, *What's He Building?*

A Pocket Guide to Trouble

i. Genesis: Making Trouble

In those first days on the job—when God was just a beginner
in a hurry, no real résumé to speak of, when finally
it was light enough for Him to see what He was doing—
surely He must have been thinking, *Don't*
let there be trouble, but He blew the line when He delivered
the official, out-loud word of God. And there was trouble.
He had all the time in the world, but no one knew yet
how long that would turn out to be. And after the backbreaking
week He'd put in already, He wasn't about to start over.

ii. The Epistemology

If it looks like trouble and it sounds like trouble
and you can't stop yourself from asking everyone you see,
What, exactly, seems to be the trouble?
then, okay, this time it's absolutely going to be trouble, or else
another one of those goddamn, less-than-obvious ducks.

iii. The Mechanics of Trouble

From the look on your face, I'm guessing it's major car trouble—
transmission, brakes, or engine. But even a cracked block is nothing,
compared to woman trouble, heart trouble that speaks for itself—
the kind that's guaranteed to really set you back: it's the labor,
not the parts. We'll get to you, one way or the other, first thing
in the morning. We'll let you know whatever we find that's not quite
beyond repair. You'll tell us what you can and can't afford.

iv. Commuters in Trouble

Odysseus found himself going to an awful lot of it
just trying to get home. Jimmy Stewart, too, near the end
of *It's a Wonderful Life*.

v. The Worst-Ever Political Advice (U.S. Edition), Expressed Here as a Trouble-Filled Couplet of Epic Proportions

Let Nixon
be Nixon.

vi. At the Border of Switzerland and Trouble

Even with millions of those red army knives and no standing army
to speak of, the Swiss have somehow managed to stay out of it.

vii. Theatrically Speaking, We've Got Trouble

right here in River City, where the Dejà-Vu-and-Blue-Hair
Community Players never seem to run out of musicals. Or else
they do. And believe me, that's trouble too—with a capital *T*
that rhymes with *D* and that stands for *Death of a Salesman*, which
they've overhauled, lightened up, led to its song-and-dance slaughter.
In the moving words of Willy Loman's wife, *Attention must be paid*—although
she sings them now in some unaccountably jaunty Calypso fashion.
Willy's thankfully still a salesman by day, but he's moonlighting as,
of all things, an amateur thespian. Every night he brings down the house,
desperately invoking his imagined former glory: *They loved me in* Oklahoma!

viii. Trouble Knows a Few Tricks

Because my novelist friend is a fan of those huge nineteenth-century novels,

he named his enormous, real-life dog Trouble, as in

Trouble climbed into bed with us this morning. Call for Trouble

and he comes. Sits. Lies down. But he won't roll over. Won't play dead

for anyone. Not as long as he still remembers every bone

he's ever buried with a real-life vengeance.

ix. What Is the Sound of Questions Getting Harder?

A Buddhist who isn't sure about the sound of two hands clapping is clearly a Buddhist already in trouble.

x. The Classic Overachiever

Jesus, facing the multitude with five loaves and two fishes
long before the advent of cole slaw as a side dish: predictably,
another miracle—no trouble at all.

xi. Sometimes Trouble Isn't on the Menu

Like decent pizza in Nebraska—by now
you should know better than to go asking for it.

xii. Like the Mountain Coming to Mohammed, Trouble

will certainly find you. It knows where you live. One of these days
the roof will spring its leak, the stove will go out for good,
the bedroom door will fall off its hinges, and the water in the toilet
won't stop running, no matter how religiously you jiggle the handle.
And suddenly trouble is an uncle with nothing better to do,
waiting up in the dark for as long as it takes you to come back.
If that's how it has to be. He's finished with following you.
He'll be easing into your favorite slippers, lifting a few fingers
of your highfalutin Scotch. He'll have you down cold—
even the nervous humming will be pitch-perfect. There's no way
you'll be able to say that you like what he's done with the place,
but you still can't help admiring how he's made himself this much at home.

xiii. (Always a Troubling Number)

Don't let that silver-haired Mr. Businessman's demeanor fool you:
Wallace Stevens was out there, bird-dogging for us all.
He knew thirteen sure-fire ways of looking for trouble, including
his favorite: shouting *Hey, you skinny, uninsured sons-of-bitches*
at the thin men of Haddam, Connecticut.

The Perfect Stranger

He saved my baby's life, then just walked away. He was a perfect stranger.
He still is.
                    —at the scene of the fire

for Patricia, eventually

No one knows how he makes his way in this imperfect world.
He doesn't have a come-on, a gimmick, or a pitch—
to say nothing of a proper name he'll own up to.
He's so good at whatever he does, it calls for no introduction.
His face is a composite of every low profile he's kept.
No perfect likeness will ever be sold as a bobblehead figurine.
He has no identifying marks. He'll never be caught dead
standing out in a crowd. If he sits down next to you at the bar,
the last thing on his mind is where have you been all his life.
He can't be out looking for that kind of trouble.
But should he come across the purse you left behind in a hurry,
you'll find it at the door in the morning, everything inside
perfectly intact, without a note of explanation. It's already more
than he really wanted to know: who you are and where you live.

By now he's in a rush of his own, all but disappearing
into one more day's white noise. But he'll be there
under a third-story window when the smoke starts pouring out
and a mother drops her baby down as softly as she can pray.
By noon he'll be at the courthouse, posting bail after unlikely bail.
His afternoon's a quintessential walk in the park—

he'll have some CPR to give. A Professor-of-Humanities Chair to endow
at a school that's gone MBA-crazy. Maybe he'd say it's nothing,
really, if only he felt like talking. What else does he have to do
except to show up where he's so completely unexpected?
It's never going to be his day to drive the office carpool.
He won't be counted on, looked forward to.

                                    Statistically speaking,
we're usually strangers ourselves, and I don't know how in the world
some days most of us are nothing if not civil to each other.
But the perfect stranger would seem to be another matter entirely.

Sometimes in his sleep he dreams up secret imperfections:
he's washing whites with colors. Forgets to turn off the lights.
Or there's a knife stuck deep in the toaster again,
mud on the dress boots or blood in the sink,
the wrong-size spoon stirring quietly in the soup.
His bid for a perfect game is spoiled by a 3-2 pitch in the dirt.
But who's he kidding? When he wakes up, there's not a chance
in hell those things will happen.

                             When I woke up today I thought
of him sitting down for breakfast, bending over a plate of eggs
cooked, of course, to perfection. And I was strangely relieved
to think he might be out there somewhere, carrying the ball
for everyone who can't quite measure up. But then again
he doesn't have anyone like you to lie down next to,
his concentration so utterly blown on a regular basis.

Surely you must know by now how often you're the reason
for these imperfect words—even when it doesn't seem that way
at first. But notice how, just four lines up, a perfect stranger
led me back to you. And he'll be out of here soon enough.
This poem actually began so long ago, it's not funny anymore.

Before the perfect stranger came to me, I was working hard
on the Moon, sweating out some Space-Race-paranoia epic, or so
I supposed. But even on the Moon I couldn't stop myself from saying
sometimes it's hard to tell apart the two extremes of love—
the giddy weightlessness, the stubborn sense of gravity. And then I said
we're better off not trying.

                    Down here the view's no less breathtaking,
and you and I get it mostly right in the long bed of our life together,
some days especially beautiful for the flaws that show up there:
how you make off to the other side with the blankets in your sleep.
How I often talk in mine, resorting to the future-perfect tense—
maybe tomorrow, next week, or more surprising years from now,
I *will have learned*, finally, to believe it when you tell me
I'm the only less-than-perfect one for you. That much still
could happen. But no doubt that's another poem completely.

And whenever I wake up that absolutely uncovered,
there's no way to pretend that we don't see
you're about to get what you've had coming all along.
That would be me, so excited that somehow I'm still flying
the flag you were raising over and over in my dream.
And I've got the whole day to explain, if I have to. Nowhere else
I'm unexpected. I already know by heart exactly who you are
and where you live and how we're about to fit together
pretty damn well, if not perfectly, one more time.

Maybe Just One Poem in This Fecund Spring Where Patricia Doesn't Suddenly Appear, Waylaying Whatever It Was I Must Have Had in Mind

for the waylayer herself

That is, if I can stop right here. Or you
decide there must be better things to do.

My plans and I were well laid way back when
I left the bed and one more night began

another poem I can't get halfway through.
Now look at what you've gone and done again.

Danse Clewellian, or: Is There a Doctor in the House?

after WCW . . . way after

If when my wife is breaking plates and tile in the basement, as always
going to so many pieces for her art, her mind's eye already fastening on
what, exactly, might become of this legion of the cracked and shattered
when pressed into service unexpectedly together,

and our pencil-wielding son is knee-deep by now in his overflowing
Comic Book of Death, laughing in the face of the very idea, drawing
his favorite conclusions: it's either the dreaded high-tech plasma beam
or that 100-ton weight no one ever sees coming out of the cartoon sky,

and his pet mouse, Jolly—so named by his original, optimistic family
that finally gave up and unloaded him here, where he's much better known as
Not-So-Jolly—is making pint-size plans for another bloodletting surprise
the next time he's sprung for his daily rodent constitutional,

and the cat is rising above the fray before it actually happens,
curling up completely in the bathroom sink, drinking all night
from the dripping faucet, and yet surely I'm the one who's somehow crazy
just for thinking I really could use a cool splash of water right now,

and I'm afraid
the Moon isn't even half-full yet
above and beyond the summer
ruckus of cicada-laden trees—

if I, overheated in my room upstairs,
undress entirely as a last resort,
grateful there's no mirror I have to answer to,
waving my THE GOVERNMENT IS LYING T-shirt about my head
and singing softly to myself:
"I am surrounded, surrounded,
I was born to be surrounded,
I am best so!"
If I admire my Charlie the Tuna lampshade, Reddy Kilowatt barbeque apron,
Bigfoot snow-globe, Dump-Nixon ashtray, Bettie Page plenty-of-action figure,
all of them on display in their own naked, oddball glory—

I'm no William Carlos Williams, but who shall say I am not
the happy captive of my household?

Meanwhile, Back at the Typewriter, I'm Hoping for a Greater Acceptance

Now that we're actually taking your work, would you be so good as to
send us copies on disk?
               —from more than one well-meaning editor's reply

I'm not sure I'll be ever *that* good. At best
I'm mostly reliable: from start to finish, a man of my typewritten word,
tooling along behind the daisy-wheel of my well-oiled Olivetti,
which has no memory to speak of—which is a blessing, given
some of the things I've rolled out of there, looking impossibly
good at 2 a.m. with no one else on the road.

Write me down as someone whose outmoded, unprocessed way with words
still makes a measurable impression, at least on paper—like Bigfoot
writ small, but indisputably heading across that snowy expanse
where anything's possible again, bringing even high-minded zoologists
to their knees: something you could point to and actually feel. This poem
would get its primordial ink on your fingers right now if it could.
It would love nothing more than to rub up against you and belong.

Hey—I sweated ampersands just finally going electric, plugging in
like Dylan at Newport, 1965, when he nearly blew the sensitive fuses
of all those acoustic-folksong purists: *I ain't gonna work*
on Maggie's farm no more. And I pounded out my own amped-up anthems,
but without the attendant booing. Without thinking for a moment
I was seriously Dylan. Beyond the desk lamp's suggestion of brilliance,

I couldn't make out a single face where an audience should have been.
There are lines, and then there are lines
I will not cross. This typewriter never fails to beep its tiny horn,
letting me know when I'm in danger of going too far.

I might yet have enough memory to include my home-phone number:
961-388-something. And if anyone bothers calling to check up on me,
I might put down the receiver right next to the *clack-clack-
clacking* of the keys—but only if the cord will stretch that far. Already
I can hear voices on the other end: *You were right, honey*—or
Smithers or *Mr. President—he doesn't have a portable phone!* And once more
I'll be a small throwback wonder, painfully quaint, as if I'd gone
and set up shop next door to the taciturn blacksmith in some colonial
Williamsburg beyond the pale of human understanding.

                                           Here's what I say:
if I'm crazy, then please be good enough to think of me as crazy
like a fox—the quick, brown beast of ancient typewriter legend,
maybe a step or two slower after so many years, but still all instinct
and optic nerve. The look in his eye is more hungry than playful
when he's jumping over the lazy dogs on his way to henhouse glory.
He needs the exercise. He's talking his typewritten way in again,
his mouth still full of feathers from the last time he was this good,
so good, almost too good to be true. And I'm not
kidding this time, either. You can take it from me.

How the Visiting Poet Ended Up in the Abandoned Nike Missile Silo in Pacific, Missouri, after Surviving a Morning of Grade-School Classroom Appearances on Behalf of One of the Better Impulses in the History of Human Behavior

i.

Because it was lunchtime, and I wasn't hungry. Because I asked
the man with the keys. And because most people had stopped asking
years ago, he gladly walked me down the road, through acres of wheat,
under the no-longer-electrifying fence to an overgrown mound of concrete
where a pair of doors, ridiculously thick, angled into the ground.
He sprang the padlocks, and then with his crowbar we pried and pulled
until those doors finally gave. He showed me down a long staircase
by flashlight until we hit bottom, standing suddenly in the middle of
another one of those it-seemed-like-a-pretty-good-idea-at-the-time
slaphappy Cold War motifs: a cavernous, unassailable bunker,
one of four whose aim was protecting St. Louis in the tenuous '50s and '60s.
Most U.S. cities *of consequence* were ringed by these underground wonders
where Nike Hercules missiles with nuclear warheads could be raised,
then guided to vaporize enemy bombers—a desperate *last line of defense*
to prevent the Russians from dropping their blood-Red nuclear cargo.
And never mind the ensuing blast, the politics and bombast,
the unavoidable fallout. Maybe, just maybe, what might be a disaster
would be visited on the boondocks alone, while the cities themselves
theoretically were saved for a more consequential future.

And I was thinking surely this was some overblown, cartoonish
opposite of the do-it-yourself backyard shelter

that Benny the Ball's father never did quite finish building in 1962.
The Ball and I would take refuge there anyway, smoking Kool
after pilfered Kool—no end of the fourth grade, not to mention
the world, that we could see. We were veterans of the weekly air-raid
drills at Hamilton School, where every kid was issued actual dog tags
so we could be identified *in case of the unthinkable*, according to
the lovely Miss Jago, our first real bombshell teacher. In case worse came
to worst. And since she'd put it that way, Miss Jago was almost all
we ever thought about. Back upstairs, bent over our desks
in the middle of New Jersey, halfway between Philadelphia and New York,
we couldn't help ourselves: yes, we were small, but we kept busy
doing the bigger arithmetic—what we most needed was more time, and then
one day our indefinite lives would finally add up to something.

ii.

Now over forty years later, he tells me he couldn't believe someone thought
it would actually work:
                    St. Louis was worth more than four of these. Hell—
Chicago had eleven. Even cow-town Kansas City had five.
                                        He was twenty
and stationed right where we stood.
                    We never knew what might happen, one day
to the next.
            In 1962, who did? Everyone's future was miles up in the air.
But he's still here—down-to-earth Senior Custodian at Nike Elementary,
a school named after a missile system. Forget about the winged
Greek goddess of victory.
                    It's nothing to do with the sneakers, either.
Just try telling those kids that the sneakers weren't until later.

The base was officially dismantled in 1967, but when he hit a certain switch
I could see the enormous lift was amazingly still in decent working order.
I could hear the power left behind in all of its ghostly hydraulics—
fifty feet of cold steel rising, humming overhead in the noontime dark.
That would bring the missiles to the surface, where they'd be loaded,
by hand, onto launchers,

                    and I was humming too, sweating it out over nothing
all over again, there in the middle of that anti-wheat, anti-Heartland,
anti-anything-that-comes-naturally-out-of-the-ground anti-silo.

Technically, the school district owns this now. That's why I have keys.
They mostly want to pretend it doesn't exist, but I keep telling them
that with a little fixing-up, they'd have one hell of a principal's office.

And me, without a hall pass. I wanted up. I really had to go. He had to laugh:
Okay, but how about a song or two before we leave? To keep our cool
we used to do a lot of singing here—Get a Job. Earth Angel.
The End of the World. *One guy's version of* High Hopes *I swear*
was better than Sinatra's.

                And before I could manage an answer,
he was every bit of twenty, breaking into *Great Balls of Fire* without warning
one more time, giving it everything he'd never truly have in him again.
Sometimes you've just got to sing your damn heart out to prove
you haven't lost it completely.

                So I struck up a few rowdy bars of Whitman.
A little pizzicato William Carlos Williams. It was strangely like singing
in some gigantic historical shower—all that unheard-of resonance—but
it would be another matter entirely back at the surface, in the wide-open
unbridled air. I'm not sure even the greatest poets ever saved so much

as a single citizen for more than a few nights at most. Let alone a city.
But with a Hercules or two behind them, I'd say all bets are off.

Some of those words sounded pretty good, but I'm here to tell you
that you can't carry a tune to save your life.

iii.

And I made it back just in time: into the sunlight, under the fence,
through the wheat, up the road to the well-oiled front door of Nike
Elementary. Because on that now-surmountable ground, someone had gone
and built a school without a basement. Because the only Warheads around
these days are nearly harmless candies, and Hercules is a cable-station
cartoon dog with the mange—although no matter what happens to him next,
at least he's wearing his tags. And because students keep showing up
all the same, dressed in T-shirts, jeans, and those inescapable sneakers.

I could have been their afternoon distraction from the daily weight
of science and history, but if these kids thought they were going
to get off as easy as the morning classes had—an hour or so of the usual
whims of whatever restless goddesses and gods, and then the inevitable
blandishments mere mortals can't help offering up in their direction,
or maybe some horses, a few headstrong flowers in winter, the red wheel
barrow, the dead deer pushed over the edge into the river at last
for the ten-thousandth time—I'm afraid they'd have another thing coming,
that afternoon and always.
              In this bad-dream age of suicide bombings,
anthrax, sleeper cells, the threat of suitcase nukes sure to be carried out
of one country for unpacking in another, even children see a deadlier world
right outside the door. Air-raid drills and guided missiles are as quaint

as home-cooked breakfast. There's no way they'll ever thrill to the sound
of an All-Clear siren in their lifetimes. They'll never know how much
some of us lived for that. Instead, they have to settle for
the bell that sends them home for another day—spared, with any luck,
from being bored to death.

        So I told them something I finally was sure of:
where human breath is so easily extinguished, taken away for good each time
by slightly different means, metaphor doesn't stand a fighting chance.
It's what they'd suspected ever since they were born—in real life, nothing
is ever unassailably enough like anything else.
        I guaranteed them
there's never been any great excuse for poems. But even at their worst,
they're not exactly weapons of mass destruction. And we can always
find them if we need to. They keep appearing, inexplicably, all over the place.
There's no telling why that is—not even here, a moment before everything
grows so unnaturally quiet, in what could have been one more sincere but
misguided attempt at a last line in their defense.

Albert Einstein Held Me in His Arms

although my parents didn't know it at the time.
And if I knew anything, even on some vaguely molecular level,
I surely wasn't talking. No one was the wiser, except
for Einstein, of course, taken with my small charms.
He was crazy about how I couldn't stop smiling,
drooling in my carriage on a Sunday afternoon in Princeton—
the town my mother loved just driving to and getting out and
losing herself in, absolutely smitten. And my pedestrian father
was crazy about my mother, so even if that meant
another goddamn trip to Highfalutinsville, New Jersey,
he'd be there without fail, forever along for the ride.

The way I finally heard it, Einstein was on his knees
in a sweatshirt, rumpled chinos, and sneakers, pulling weeds—
Merely being himself, my father would say later, utterly impressed.
Einstein had that down to a science at 112 Mercer, the unassuming
white-frame house where he cultivated flowers, where he played the violin
precisely in sync with his favorite recordings late into the night.
Where he famously met with Bertrand Russell, Kurt Gödel, and Wolfgang Pauli
for philosophic forays into the schnapps, then inevitably higher mathematics.
But on that one historic Sunday in the spring of my first year,
Einstein himself welcomed the unrenowned likes of my mother and father.
This twentieth-century giant picked me up with some easy peekaboo small talk
in the last of the afternoon's fading light until, eventually, genius
or no genius, I couldn't take it anymore, and I made a tiny grab

for his wildly theoretical hair. And that was pretty much the end
of our ad hoc civilization that flourished for ten Princeton minutes.

When Einstein died only six weeks later,
every newspaper ran his picture, and all at once my father
couldn't believe it: *Wasn't that the gardener who couldn't get enough*
of the baby? It says right here he's Einstein,
the guy who revolutionized our thinking about time and space!
And what was that supposed to mean to him, exactly? My father
wasn't Einstein, but he'd thought a lot about time and space, too,
deciding in his lifetime he wasn't about to get enough of either one.

For years my parents never said a word about that day, as if
to remember it out loud would have been somehow unseemly—
a kind of bragging they never much went in for—rather than a celebration
of wonderful dumb-luck Sunday driving, like every happy accident
in the history of science or in those classic, unlikely stories
we can't help going back to for their mythic staying power. So now let me
put it this way: Albert Einstein held me in his arms before he died.

Sooner or later we're all trying to explain our particle selves
in light of our own outlandish theories of relativity.
Someone in my family—my mother or my father, maybe me—
had to embellish at least some of the truth that comes, finally,
here at the end:
                    my mother's horrified
that I've yanked poor Einstein's hair, and she resigns herself,
sighing *It's time to go.* To prove there are no hard feelings,
he says something Einsteinian, like *Yes, but what is time?*—
which my father misunderstands as a question he can actually answer
at that very minute, so he says *five o'clock.* And before I know it,
because I am far too young to realize much of anything,

everyone's in a sudden hurry back into their uncertain futures,
as if this whole thing never quite honestly happened, and in no time
it's fifty years later, and I'm the one still alive, all that's left
of the story, telling myself: Yes, it did. No, it didn't. No, it did.

IV

Jack Ruby's America

See the man with the stage fright
just standin' up there to give it all his might.
He got caught in the spotlight,
but when we get to the end
he wants to start all over again.
    —The Band, *Stage Fright*

Suddenly I'm in a world of history.
    —Jack Ruby

I. Jack Ruby Orders the Chicken Salad: November 21, 1963

You know how I need it, Sweetheart: all my orders are To Go.
I'm the king of Carry-Out. Today I'm good for a dozen—half rye,
half rolls. These are heading down to the station, so pile it on
a little thick, okay? They know me there. I'm a regular
no-baloney guy making sure the cops get a decent shot at lunch.
You can't say I don't love Dallas, but still: give me Chicago
for cold cuts a man like me could die for—hot pastrami, corned beef,
tongue that doesn't quit. I go for sandwiches in a big way, a handful
of good will folks can sink their teeth into. And people remember
certain things. Don't get me started on how crazy it is sometimes
to be me, in Texas. But then I've always liked going out of my way

if it lets me in on the action. When you're the one with sandwiches,
you let other people do the talking. Just look who's talking now,
right? I need sandwiches, I'm friendlier. So to speak. Human nature,
if you ask me. I've studied it. I'm talking my whole life. Go ahead
and ask me is there anything I don't know about human nature. I'm here
to tell you mostly it's not much: I'm talking one sorry load
of chicken salad sandwiches bagged up in the front seat of a car
in the Dallas sun. At noon. You know it won't be long before
it goes completely bad. And we're Texas, down here so Deep
in the Heart that it's never been lip-smacking good to begin with.

So what do I finally owe you? Here's a twenty. Keep the change
and get yourself something later. Something you've always been

meaning to. On me. I'm talking something extra: a little bit
of trouble or excitement you don't really need. That we can live
without either one, thank you, is no good reason. I'm talking America,
getting whatever we deserve. Human nature: remember that. Remember me
to the rest of the shift. I'll be back. I'm always coming back.
And next time, you can cut the *Mister* jazz. Jack is good enough.

II. The Chicago Cowboy

I have read from stories of personalities that are notorious. That is the extent of my involvement in any criminal activity.
—Ruby, to Earl Warren (1964)

We could not establish a significant link between Ruby and organized crime.
—The Warren Commission Report

It was 1947. Jack heard he'd be getting a call.
After all these Windy City years, it was surely his time to go West
and he was thinking *Los Angeles*, maybe *Vegas*. He was thinking
he was that important: finally they'd let him have his own piece
of some sophisticated action. When the word came down
he'd be heading to Dallas, Jack couldn't believe someone had him
all wrong. His talents would be wasted in a nowhere town like that.
The Chicago Boys smelled Texas oil, and they were looking
to control the wide-open gambling scene. They thought of Jack
as a man who could handle the chump change, and would he please
be good enough to dole it out as needed, making fast friends
with the Dallas police?
                              They promised he'd feel bigger down there,
and Jack had to admit he liked the sound of that, even if
down there was some kind of joke. He'd suck it in. He'd zip it up.
He'd be their Chicago Cowboy, as long as he got his.
He'd ask them to spring for a little velvet, something jazzy
in a white snap-brim hat. He could show them good, but
they shouldn't count on Jack anymore to be that good for nothing.

Sixteen years later there's not much left for Jack to think about:
the Carousel Club, 1312½ Commerce. The half's because he's one flight up,
where rent's a little lower. The stenciled message on the stairway wall,
A FEW STEPS CLOSER TO HEAVEN, wasn't Jack's idea. The single
rectangular room wasn't quite the place he'd hoped for, either.
He'd dreamed of a sumptuous club-in-the-round, slowly revolving
on the top floor of a tower, where some kind of breathtaking view
was just a reservation away.

                    Still, by his peculiar standards,
he's made the most of it: jet-black booths, dark red carpeting,
gold mesh curtains. Over the bar, a squadron of gold crowns
hanging from the ceiling—Jack liked the idea of working around those.
From the moment he first walked in and took over the operation,
he could see it wasn't called the Sovereign for nothing.
And one enormous black-velvet painting of a well-hung stallion in gold.
Jack guaranteed the bartender who helped him nail it to the wall:
The 3-D effect is what makes it real class. His favorite word,
class, is all he wants to be known for. This wouldn't be a *joint*,
but a *nightclub*. And his girls would be *dancers, hostesses,
entertainers*. Truly a man ahead of his euphemistic time, this Sultan
of Schmooze, this Kibitzer King, with his homespun sense of nobility.
And this is his low-rent kingdom. Welcome to the house
that Jack built: *If they complain about the two-dollar cover,
tell them it's worth it just for an eyeful of the décor. We're fucking
class on top of class in here.*

                    ———◆✦✦◆———

Before making a go of the Carousel: the Silver Spur. The Ranch House.
Hernando's Hideaway. Then enough of the Texas motifs. Let's try
the Vegas. And, of course, the Sovereign. Jack had a rapid succession
of dreams that didn't stick. But this is the one he can't seem
to shake: the Carousel, sandwiched between the Weinstein brothers'
Colony Club and the Theatre Lounge—where every night is Amateur Night
and the Weinsteins have got Jack fuming. He's the one paying
for professional talent, trying to keep up some thin veneer of class.
He's been known to travel out of town just to recruit it.
He's still trying to live up to the good name he's made for himself.
Jacob Rubenstein's no proper name for a night-spot operator.
The reporters and cops come here to hang with Jack Ruby, club owner,
producer, dispenser of small favors: free drinks any time.

———◆•▸◀•◆———

If you ask Jack, he just can't help thinking of Dallas
as one gigantic Amateur Night. In his heart it's never been a city.
Back when Chicago was nearly wiped out by fire, Dallas was barely
on the map, too green to burn. It's still too new. There's no fire,
there's nothing *neighborhood* about it, and Jack is neighborhood
all the way: do-for-you, do-for-me. No questions. No problem.
He learned his lessons on solid concrete stoops, along miles
of narrow fire escapes, in tenement backyard clothes-flapping breezes
where any street worth its name had something new to teach you,
like how you could finally manage to stand to your own full height
and deliver. Even as a sawed-off kid, Sparky Rubenstein delivered:
sealed envelopes, a buck an errand, for Capone's associates.
He pushed key chains, bottle openers, knives from a cart. Scalped tickets
outside Soldier Field, hustled peanuts during the game. He sold himself
on helping others: tip sheets at the races. Carnations in the dancehalls.
Awful chocolates in the burleyque's raucous dark.

———◆◆◆◆———

Jack believes in what he insists on calling his orchestra:
four sorry tuxedos sitting at the back of an otherwise naked stage.
Ever since the night a musician bit off the tip of Jack's finger,
there's been no love lost between Jack and the music. Still, he wants
to do it up right. He's always looking for any cut above.
More clothes are coming off to the sound of rock 'n' roll records
all over town. But where Jack's the master of ceremonies,
he wants everything live.

He's making his uneasy way through the crowd
with a microphone in his hand, when *bang*, out of nowhere:
the drummer's rim-shot. And good evening, he's our host, Jack Ruby,
and we're not going to believe what he's planned for us this time.

———◆◆◆———

The best music Jack ever heard was in Havana.
When he squeezes shut his eyes just right, he can still see
the dazzling lights of the Tropicana after sundown. Now, that
was a nightclub, cabaret, casino supreme—room after room
of posh and glitz. No other action in the world came even close.
In exchange for delivering some crates of unnumbered rifles and guns,
Jack shot the Caribbean breeze with the wheels of the operation:
Santo Trafficante, Carlos Marcello, and his particular heroes,
Meyer Lansky and brother Jake. As long as Batista could hold on,
there would be the fabled Tropicana, where the insignificant likes
of Abe and Barney Weinstein would be spots on the silverware.
Everyone at the table knew what was coming if Castro moved in to stay:
there goes the glittering neighborhood.

But no one can take it away
from Jack now: his few days in the Cuban sun, the bloody steaks
a cut above, the umbrella drinks he never touched, but he liked how
they were there for him. Trafficante himself nearly busting a gut
when Jack played Conway Twitty air guitar on *It's Only
Make Believe*. And Jack soaked it in, he ate it all up, this living
at last high off the hog, an honorary Kosher Nostra boy.

———◆·›‹·◆———

This afternoon Jack's in his tiny Carousel office,
and his head is spinning. Along with the gun-metal-grey desk,
beat-up easy chair, and the hand-lettered sign on the wall—SHOW
SOME CLASS—now there's a safe Jack's actually had installed.
For the man who's always kept his cash in brown paper sandwich bags
or wadded thick in his pockets, who's never had a checkbook,
who never cracks a smile when he calls his money *dough*,
this may take some serious getting used to. He's on the phone,
letting his attorney know he's just in from the Tropicana
in Vegas, and he's got the simoleons to pay off his back taxes.
And Jack is nearly giddy, for Jack. He's off the hook again.
He can keep his doors wide open for the indefinite future.

They'd told him it was the least they could do, a small 40-grand
favor he should consider more of a thank-you for all the years
in the Texas sun. For being there.
                          And for a minute
he almost dreams himself out of his cash-and-carry life. *Jack's
good for it* is what they'd said. For Dallas. For business.
For the long green. Somewhere out West he's sure he could be
a real nightclub operator. A-listed partygoer. Fedora sensation.
Confidant to the stars.
                          But there's no time off for good behavior
in the Lone Star State, and the Chicago Cowboy will be right back
where he's always been: would-be high roller in a rumpled suit,
in precarious business for himself again
a few steps short of Heaven. 1312½ Commerce—halfway between
the police station and the county jail. *A rock-and-a-hard-place
kind of thing*, he jokes nightly at the mike. The cops drink free
and barely pay attention. But except for the Weinstein brothers,
Jack's never minded being in the middle. If there's any action.

So plug him in and light him up. Full of his misguided sense
of decorum, he's about to go out there again and try shooting off
his mouth full of cornball gratitude in front of another crowd
that isn't here to listen. They've paid their deuce apiece
for *Girls! Girls! Girls!* and who's Jack Ruby to insinuate himself
into such a straightforward arrangement?

                                                 He's learned one thing
over and over again in his obligated life: there's no way
he can really help himself.

III. Jack Ruby Talks Business with the New Girl: November 21, 1963

I will say this only once to you, I promise: business
is business. It's nothing personal. All business
is good business. You heard of selling the sizzle,
not the steak? Be sure you're only sizzle. Nothing but.
They're hungrier than that, they can beat it somewhere else.
I run this place so clean, some nights people hear it squeak.

Smile all you want, but no life stories, ever. I never knew
a smile that hurt, but keep your real name to yourself.
And when you hear whatever name you're going by tonight,
it's your turn to dance. And you dance. With class. Like
nobody's business. You make your entrance, hit your mark,
and get it done. And let's face it: the music
isn't much. But it's all yours. Do what you can.

And somebody thinks he knows how to soften you up with sweet
talk or a roll of bills, remember: you always know better.
This is no business to make that kind of mistake in.
Take it from me: you don't want to walk into anything
you can't talk your innocent-enough way out of.

And if there's trouble you didn't see coming, don't worry.
That's what I'll be out there looking for. I may be incognito,
just another hat in the crowd. But if you want to know the truth,
all you have to do is ask. You say *Jack* and I swear

I'll come through. Say the word, and some guy's good as dead.
He'll learn fast: guys like him are our business, and who we are

is really none of his. As long as you're working for me,
you're covered. Partners. No matter how it has to mostly seem.
Yeah, you're the one who's out there at point-blank range,
but I will never leave you twisting in the wind, whichever way
it's blowing that night, alone in any of this business.

IV. The Difference a Day Makes

You guys all know me. I'm Jack Ruby.
> —to the policemen who wrestled him to the floor after
> he shot Oswald

You can get more out of me. Let's not break up too soon. I have been used for a
purpose, but it can't be said here. Unless you get me to Washington, you can't get a fair
shake out of me. Dallas is a homicidal town.
> —Ruby, to Earl Warren

When the motorcade hits Dealey Plaza, Jack's five blocks away
at the *Dallas Morning News*, placing an ad for the Carousel.
He'd be at the parade, but he's already pushing the paper's
Friday-at-noon deadline, and these days he has to pay up front
for everything. In the composing room a portable TV can barely contain
the breaking news. Jack can't believe anyone would whack a president
in this kind of broad daylight.
He's stunned but undeniably
excited, racing to Parkland Hospital. He always knows the shortest route
to any spectacle in Dallas. There's bound to be some serious action
going down there, and he wants to be one of the first to find out
if Kennedy's going to make it. And if not, should he close his club—
it would be the gentlemanly, graceful thing to do—
and for how many goddamn nights?

He's there in time to hear the doctor pronouncing death. *A black eye*
for the city, Jack says to the man standing next to him. And why
does it have to be the weekend, when things are smoking most

in his business? A Saturday is worst of all to lose.

His ad's already paid for, true, but surely for Jack Ruby

they can turn it into something more respectful: *Closed* or *In Memoriam*.

Whatever's classy. He's up to his neck in this historic moment:

no club he's put over half his heart or money into voluntarily

has been dark for even a single night. He hopes those unpatriotic

Weinstein brothers in their greed stay open for everyone to see.

It's way past dark when Jack makes one of his trademark stops
at Phil's Delicatessen: a dozen corned beef sandwiches, a dozen
bottles of celery tonic. He's jawing to the counterman: *In my mind*
suddenly it mulled over me that the police were working overtime.
So to speak. An impossibly detailed description of the suspect,
Oswald, was circulating scant minutes after the fatal shots were fired.
Seventy-five minutes later, he's hauled out of a movie theatre,
a matinee showing of Audie Murphy's *War Is Hell,* and this day in Dallas
has been that kind of war: president assassinated, governor wounded,
a mail-order rifle and shell casings found in the Book Depository,
an Officer Tippit gunned down miles from Dealey Plaza, supposedly
with a mail-order Smith & Wesson .38 in the hands of this scrawny,
omnipresent 24-year-old ex-Marine. And something about Russia
and Fair Play for Cuba, and Jack is still waiting for his order
and thinking out loud *it's in-fucking-credible,* how fast
they're fitting all these pieces together. How much news there really is.
And foot soldier Jack wants in before this war is over. He's not too proud
to buy his usual position up at the frontline. From way back
he's been an enlisted man with a bad haircut, but he can dream,
can't he: *No shit, it's been a nightmare, Phil. And my goddamn feet*
are killing me. He means this day in Dallas, how it just doesn't quit.

———◆◆◆◆◆———

Jack steps off the elevator at midnight, and cockeyed luck is with him:
he's being swept along through the crowded hall to the Dallas PD's
basement assembly room where Oswald's about to be put on display
so the rumors that this prisoner's been in any way manhandled
can be laid to rest. In this blur of wingtip shoes that's passing
for history's forward momentum, no one's about to stop Jack Ruby.

In his dark suit and customary snap-brim, Jack could almost be
a plainclothes detective. He's standing on a table in the back,
craning his neck, making notes like a reporter. He could be mistaken
for either one, and for the moment he's having it both ways:
the time of his imaginary life. He's correcting the district attorney
who's just mentioned Oswald and Castro and a "Free Cuba Committee"—
that's Fair Play for Cuba Committee. Don't these guys ever listen
at least to the news? And now comes his first good look at Oswald
himself: he seems so small, so lost in this crowd, as if
he'd be a lot happier right now giving a souped-up Chevy the gas
and gunning down Main Street until there's nothing but the day ahead.
Even his matter-of-fact I'm a patsy is all but swallowed up
in this ricochet of questions, the crossfire of self-congratulation.

And no matter where he finds himself, this is Jack's time of night.
A few more minutes, and Oswald's gone. Show's over, but Jack
is in no big hurry to leave. He likes being awake at this hour
with his usual roll of cash and loaded snub-nose in his pocket.
And this evening's no exception. Yes, he should be considered armed
but not real dangerous tonight. He's pressing the flesh
with the out-of-town reporters, handing out his "Jack Ruby, Your Host
at the Carousel" calling cards, and they should try to stick around
a few days, he can make it worth their time. The drinks are on him
when the club reopens, when all the Dallas hoopla finally dies down
and Jack can make it his business again to give folks a little

something they can't get at home: *a taste of pizzazz and a shot of hubba-hubba.* And when the reporters ask can they quote him on that, he says of course, he does it all the time himself.

———◆◆◆◆◆———

Jack's too wound-up to sleep. His heart is thumping to a tune
he can't begin to carry. Especially not here at 4 a.m., but at least
Friday's over in America. Officially, it's a new day that finds Jack
in the main office of the *Dallas Times Herald*, showing off
his latest sure-fire get-rich-quick scheme—the Twist-Ercizer,
a five-dollar exercise gimmick based on what's left of the dance craze:
a platform the size of a bathroom scale, set on seventy ball bearings.
Jack steps up, and he swivels. He shimmies. He's turning in every
direction at once, a squat 180 pounds of wobbling, centrifugal force.
He's trying to get dibs on its national distribution,
so are there any questions he can answer, how many are they good for.
He's in a crowded smoke-filled room again, but this time Jack
is the only reason. These people need some kind of relief about now.
A few of them are laughing until they hurt, until it only looks like
crying. They never knew what this guy was going to think of next.
And Jack's laughing too, like there's no tomorrow. He needs buyers
right now for whatever he's selling. He can't keep spinning this way
forever. Another night's taking a sharp turn into the next morning
in the middle of his life, and Jack's still going.
He's hanging on. He's trying not to lose his balance.

———◆◆◆◆◆———

Jack's collapsed on his living room sofa
in whatever version of sleep sheer nervous exhaustion allows him.
Something happened this Saturday afternoon that turned him around
and upside down, bringing out the hangdog he keeps shut up inside
his garrulous, showboating self. He hasn't done anything yet,
but he's hiding out finally where no one would ever think to look.
Jack Ruby is unbelievably home, and he's holing up here until morning.

He shouldn't have answered the phone ringing off the hook at the Carousel.
He was only there because where else is he supposed to be.
This time the police were looking for him. They were actually asking
for the pleasure of his company. They were passing down the word
that sounded suspiciously like the word that sent him from Chicago
to Dallas in the first place. And Jack has forty thousand reasons why
he'll still be good enough. If he doesn't get it done, he's as good
as dead, he's got a feeling, stranded and uncelebrated forever
in Dallas. Maybe this can be at last his parting shot, his ticket out.
With no warning, he's in way over his head. But he's *in*, goddammit,
he's in.
        And in a flash he sees who the cops are working for.
He can only imagine the months of rehearsing that went into this
One Show Only in Dealey Plaza. The only flub, apparently, was Oswald,
who never understood his part to begin with—one more hapless actor
asking whoever's directing, *What's my motivation?* Now he's absolutely
off the script, and who knows what he'll say with the cameras rolling.

So here's where Jack comes in: last-minute bit-part addition, a walk-on
to end all walk-ons. And he can be a real quick study when he has to.
It's the weekend's sudden acceleration: in a matter of seconds Jack goes
from knowing zero to knowing just enough to be dangerous tomorrow.
He'd rather be smack in the middle of another Carousel Saturday night,
bouncing some unruly asshole down the stairs if he had to, okay,

but that guy would always manage to pick himself up off the ground
and get on with the rest of his no-account life.

———◆◆×◆◆———

Jack's turning over and over in his sleep. There's no way he'll ever
get comfortable tonight. Maybe it's just another bad dream: this owner
he knew years ago from a competing club is slashed bad in a fight.
Jack hustles down to Parkland again to donate some of his own blood.
And when the guy wakes up, there's Jack at his bedside,
shaking his head and whispering, *Well, I guess we're partners now.*
Jack's always taken pride in working alone, but he can't tell
if the Jack in the dream is only kidding.
                                        And it's getting all mixed up
with the episode of *Gunsmoke* on the TV Jack never turned off.
Now he's in a crowded saloon, pushing past Marshal Matt Dillon
and his gimpy-legged deputy, Chester B. Goode. He's looking around
desperately for the high sign from some flunky at the bar, but
before the bad guy of the week can make it through the swinging doors,
Miss Kitty smiles and drops her skirt, and everyone in the place can see
she's packing enough heat to kill any man several times over. And Jack
is sweating a lot by now. He's reaching deep into his pocket
for one of his Carousel cards. He needs a new headliner with genuine
star power, some undeniable class, and they should discuss what's possible
after whichever one of them gets to Oswald first.

                                    This whole thing
could turn out all right, he's guessing. In the bargain there's a chance
he could be treated like some kind of hero. And he'd be saving Jackie
the emotional expense of coming back to Dodge for the trial. He can almost
see it now: there goes the Chicago Cowboy riding off into the credits,
heading north again into a long winter of television snow.

—◆•☩•◆—

The good people of Dallas are going to church or, forgivably,
staying home this one Sunday to watch the TV coverage of America's
ceremonial grief. Today the cortège will leave the White House,
making its darker, anti-motorcade way up Pennsylvania Avenue
to the Capitol Rotunda. There's not a chance Jack's staying home
to be any part of that. He waited hours by his phone for someone to call
this whole thing off, but he's long gone now. He's been to Western Union
wiring money to his pregnant dancer in Fort Worth. The entire Carousel crew
except for Jack is out of work for the weekend, and Little Lynn especially
could use the tiding over. Jack's hoping to use his generosity later
as the reason he's downtown at all coincidentally with his cash
and a loaded gun. Wherever he is right now, he's only protecting himself.
He's carrying two thousand dollars. He's wired Lynn twenty-five bucks.
His Western Union receipt says *11:17*, and he'll say he wasn't even thinking
about the police station one block away until he finished his transaction
and figured it was Sunday, what the hell, he had a little extra
time to kill and his surplus curiosity and how's he supposed to know
that the ballyhooed 10 a.m. transfer of Oswald from the city lock-up
to the county jail had been delayed. Let them all think Jack's too late
for any premeditation. This is his only chance: it's got to play out
as a stroke of dumb luck—good or bad, depending as always
on where you're standing. *Spontaneous* is the word he's looking for.

━━━◆◈◆━━━

Jack's walking down from Western Union to the station right now.
The Preludin he's swallowed no doubt quickens his step. He'll be there
in ninety seconds. Not that Jack really needs the extra stimulation,
but for months he's been telling his doctor all the good it does him:
*I'm a positive thinker. I don't have any inferiority, and my reflexes
are fan-fucking-tastic.* And Jack is positive no one's going anywhere
quite yet. Finally there's a party in Dallas that won't be starting
without him.

        He's wearing a white shirt, black silk tie, his best
charcoal-brown suit, black shoes, and grey fedora. Pretty spiffy
for nothing more than a casual errand. He knows exactly where he's been
headed all along. This is one of Jack's special detective get-ups.
He read a sidebar in yesterday's paper: in 1901 the Buffalo, New York police,
worried about a hostile crowd, sneaked out President McKinley's assassin
by dressing him as a cop. Surely Jack can turn that around with ease.
He's practically an honorary cop already, so what
could it hurt to take that approach himself today, sneaking in.

Appearances are deceiving, but only if you're willing to work at them.
Jack bathes and shaves twice daily. It's like getting one more crack
at the same gritty day. He pampers his skin with lotions and creams.
He swims and works out when he can at the Y. He's always operated
on the notion that what's on the outside makes or breaks a person
in this world. What's inside may be an entirely different story,
and even that one changes a little every time it's told.

———◆━◆━◆———

What's inside Jack's white, two-door 1960 Oldsmobile this morning:
two sets of metal knuckles, the holster for his pistol, a paper bag
stuffed with another thousand dollars, a stash of unpaid parking tickets.
Several white handkerchiefs, for the show of sweat Jack always manages
doing the simplest things. A white bathing cap, a left golf shoe,
a roll of toilet paper, one can of paint, a Lo-Cal chocolate shake.
Days of newspapers full of Kennedy's impending visit, but folded open
to the pages with the nightclub ads. A notebook listing the names
and numbers of cops with lifetime free passes to the Carousel.
And Sheba, Jack's beloved dachshund, who goes everywhere with him—
to work, back home, to favorite all-night restaurants: *I call her
my wife. We argue and we make the hell up.* She's his stroke-of-genius
ace in the premeditation hole: no one would believe he'd ever leave her
waiting in the car unless really he had no idea what he was about to do.
Part of him doesn't believe it himself, and it's all he can do to walk away
and not look back.

        But the main thing Jack hopes anyone would notice
is the snazzy wash-and-wax job. As far as he's concerned today,
anything beyond that is no one else's business. Anybody's guess.

———◆✦◆———

This morning Jack's getting in free. When he arrives
in the basement garage at 11:19, he hears a car horn honking
from the top of the exit ramp its *shave-and-a-haircut, two bits.*
A phone call goes up to the third floor, where Oswald's squirming
into the sweater he'll wear for the transfer: everything's in place below,
it's time to put this show into motion. But truthfully, so much is utterly
out of place: reporters are hopelessly mixed in with police,
who are supposed to fall into a protective human corridor formation
when Oswald's finally escorted to what they're calling the getaway car
for his painstaking ride back to Dealey Plaza and the county jail
twelve risky blocks from here. And that car's nowhere in position
at the bottom of the ramp, but Jack is: no badge, no press credentials,
but he's on official business nonetheless, and the cops have let him
get this far at least in this roughhouse ballet of synchronized movements.

This is going like dimestore clockwork:
Oswald's coming down in the elevator, Jack's moving along the railing,
one hand in his pocket, the other at the brim of his fedora.
The klieg lights have cast everyone down here in the their most unflattering light,
and Jack's trying hard to concentrate on his small piece of the action.
He'll have only a single take to hit his mark, deliver, and get lost.

———◆⭑❋⭑◆———

And Oswald's off the elevator, headed toward the cameras.

He's walking Jack's way, expressionless,

a detective on his left arm, another manacled to his right wrist

and it's just a crazy, fleeting thought, but Jack can't help thinking

what a sharp cut of cream-colored suit the handcuffed detective's wearing.

The gun's out of his pocket by now and he's pushing irretrievably forward

a few more feet until there's nothing between himself and Oswald

in his crummy thrift-store sweater that can possibly save them.

And Jack's holding his arm straight out as if he's about to hand over

a gift or ask for an autograph, but instead there's this irrevocable

pop as he unloads his single shot at point-blank range.

———◆◆◆———

Two men have just gone down so close together in the crowd that at first
it's hard telling who's who, but one of them is smaller, down for good.
They're giving him artificial respiration—the worst idea in the world,
considering where that sudden bullet's lodged. They're doing their best
to restrain the other man, giving him some half-assed third-degree,
as if he's really listening. The last he knew, he's among friends here.
He's pissed they've knocked him down, and where's his fedora, this isn't
the way he pictured it going. They're treating Jack Ruby like a perfect
stranger in their midst, and there's a sickening feeling coming on
strong in Jack's stomach, too. He's only trying to get away
with the rest of his life, but not so fast: there are still too many
questions, and no one's going anywhere but down again today.

V. Jack Ruby Spends His Last New Year's Eve with His Sister, Telling the Truth as He Knows It: Parkland Hospital, December 31, 1966

So ask me how many times did I know anything, really,
in this life. Ask me did anyone ever bother handing over
anything I could use. These days almost no one recognizes me.
Up here on the sixth floor, I'm Jack Shit in a bathrobe.
And the doctors making their hypodermic rounds are claiming
everything's for the pain, as if that's what they're trying to get rid of.
I'm not supposed to realize they're delivering more of the cancer
because obviously someone out there still thinks enough of me
to want me gone, especially now with my conviction overturned,
and instead of getting the Chair I'm down for a new trial out of town,
somewhere that isn't Dallas. These last three years that's all
I've asked for: let's go someplace else and talk. I should live
so long. I'd say a few things so good, they'd stay said that way
forever. Three years go by, and I'm not your same brother. I'm related
to history now, condemned to keep repeating myself until someone finally
listens. I want to put things right. But not here.

After that sorry Oswald collapsed, I admitted doing it
to show the world that Jews have guts. Or *to spare the widow Jackie*
another trip to Dallas. At the time, I was shooting for *impulsive*
or *sympathetic*—reasons enough, it turns out, to convict me anyway.
But now someone's decided anything I said clearly should have been
inadmissible. My lawyer Belli tried to sell the jury I'm a victim
of psycho-something epilepsy—*all you need to know is* blackouts, *Jack.*
Hell, I wouldn't buy that myself if Jesus Christ was giving it away

on the courthouse steps. It took the jury less than an hour
to figure of course I'm guilty, and what else could they say.
No one in that courtroom was expecting an order of death, but that's
what the jury recommended. I could have gone for something lighter
that early in the morning. Death seemed a little much.

Real guts would have been telling Marcello's guys to shoot their craps
in hell when they called me of all people, wanted me to know
some unsuspecting putz I'd never heard of in my life had failed
to leave the country fast enough or else—
by sheer coincidence, you understand—get taken out himself. Instead,
he'd been brought in by the wrong cops, unexpectedly
alive. Lee Fucking Oswald—another one of history's three-name nut jobs.
And I could feel it slipping away, that moment
he was still their unfortunate problem more than he was mine.
They were thanking me already for remembering who
I should gladly thank for being still alive in the nightclub business.
And this is when I figure out what's going on for myself: it's not
some half-cocked flake on the loose by himself in Dealey Plaza.
And this is when I know I've got to take the play. If I don't,
all kinds of things get taken from me, fast.
And I know people in this town who would never be able to get enough
of that: *Yessirreee . . . hitting a Catholic boy's not bad at all,
but can we still get us a Jew?*

                I came out of fucking nowhere,
and I've been working my way back ever since. But there's no way
I'm about to die even close to guilty in the eyes of the law.
I've been reversed for two months now, and it's as if what happened
never happened—my part of it, at least. I'm almost beside the point.
I said it before: I'm history. I'll stay written down forever
in the Warren Commission Report. Twenty-six books it took those guys

to dish out all the bullshit required to conclude what they already
had in their made-up minds to begin with: *Oswald. Only Oswald.*
Once they've got that down cold, the *Ruby, only Ruby* part's a snap.

I've got my own Magic Bullet Theory, and this one you can take
to the bank. It's not any single shot zigzagging through Kennedy
and Connally, opening seven wounds and breaking bones along the way
before finally emerging as Warren Commission Exhibit 399 when it's found
hours later, pristine on a stretcher here at Parkland.
                                               My theory says
it's the bullet all of us have to bite, sooner or later, like our lives
depend on it—a kind of making do, getting by this shaky way
or that, even if we'd rather not. It's nothing that goes through us
and comes out clean on the other side. It's whatever we have to go through,
ourselves, at midnight or high noon. With no one watching.
And when a few minutes go by, or days, or years of actually feeling
free, in the clear, like we've dodged another round of trouble and maybe
we can get back to business as usual: here comes that unmistakable bullet
with our name on it again. Just like in the cartoons, now it's changing
directions, about to hit us one more time in the ass. And that means
one more time we'll have to swear we never saw it coming.

So Happy Fucking New Year, Sis. How about you try the Ritz
or maybe Phil's for some pastrami, corned beef on rye with a few extra
kosher dills. Bagels and cream cheese, lox and green onions. I say
bring it all on. This is still America, last time I checked,
and who knows. Maybe I'm still strong enough to keep a lot of it down.
You tell them you're there for Jack Ruby. And how much
I appreciate that. Tell them make it lean, because Jack Ruby did everybody
at least one favor in his life. Tell them what I told you:
more than ever, I'm history. But I was there for them, too.
And if your order's not completely on the house after all of that,

you tell them, if it's not asking for too damn much,
for all the business your brother's done his part to keep them in,
maybe he could get finally a little credit this one time.
Only make it sound better, okay? Make me sound better. Not so small.
You're so good to me, it hurts. Play it however you want to,

but you never even thought about any of this, let alone discussed it
with me or anyone else, until you saw that, to your surprise,
they were still open on New Year's Eve. And you walked through the door.